U.S. Department of Transportation
Federal Aviation Administration

FAA-S-ACS-8C
Includes FAA-G-ACS-2

T0015145

Airman Certification Standards
Instrument Rating
Airplane

AVIATION SUPPLIES & ACADEMICS, INC.
NEWCASTLE, WASHINGTON

Instrument Rating Airplane Airman Certification Standards

Aviation Supplies & Academics, Inc.
7005 132nd Place SE
Newcastle, Washington 98059
asa@asa2fly.com | 425-235-1500 | asa2fly.com

Visit asa2fly.com/acsupdates for FAA revisions affecting this title.

None of the material in this book supersedes any operational documents or procedures issued by the Federal Aviation Administration.

ASA-ACS-8C
ISBN 978-1-64425-450-9

Additional formats available:
eBook EPUB   ISBN 978-1-64425-451-6
eBook PDF   ISBN 978-1-64425-452-3

Printed in the United States of America

2028 2027 2026 2025 2024   9 8 7 6 5 4 3 2 1

Contents

U.S. Department
of Transportation

**Federal Aviation
Administration**

FAA-S-ACS-8C

Instrument Rating – Airplane
Airman Certification Standards

November 2023

Flight Standards Service
Washington, DC 20591

Foreword

The U.S. Department of Transportation, Federal Aviation Administration (FAA), Office of Safety Standards, Regulatory Support Division, Airman Testing Standards Branch, has published the Instrument Rating – Airplane Airman Certification Standards (ACS) to communicate the aeronautical knowledge, risk management, and flight proficiency standards for the Instrument Rating in the airplane category.

This ACS is available for download, in PDF format, from www.faa.gov.

Comments regarding this ACS may be emailed to acsptsinquiries@faa.gov.

The FAA created FAA-G-ACS-2, Airman Certification Standards Companion Guide for Pilots, to provide guidance considered relevant and useful to the community. The number of appendices in the ACS was reduced and much of the non-regulatory material was moved to the Airman Certification Standards Companion Guide for Pilots. Applicants, instructors, and evaluators should consult this companion guide to familiarize themselves with ACS procedures. FAA-G-ACS-2 is available for download, in PDF format, from www.faa.gov.

Revision History

Document #	Description	Date
FAA-S-8081-4E	Instrument Rating Practical Test Standards for Airplane, Helicopter, and Powered Lift (with Changes 1-5)	January 2010
FAA-S-ACS-8	Instrument Rating Airplane Airman Certification Standards	June 1, 2016
FAA-S-ACS-8	Instrument Rating Airplane Airman Certification Standards (Change 1)	June 15, 2016
FAA-S-ACS-8A	Instrument Rating – Airplane Airman Certification Standards	June 12, 2017
FAA-S-ACS-8B	Instrument Rating – Airplane Airman Certification Standards	June 11, 2018
FAA-S-ACS-8B	Instrument Rating – Airplane Airman Certification Standards (with Change 1)	June 6, 2019
FAA-S-ACS-8C	Instrument Rating – Airplane Airman Certification Standards	November 2023

Major Enhancements to FAA-S-ACS-8C

- The following ACS codes have been added:

IR.I.B.K2a	IR.I.C.K1d	IR.III.B.S3a	IR.V.A.S10
IR.I.B.K2b	IR.I.C.K1e	IR.IV.B.K3	IR.VI.A.S15
IR.I.B.K2c	IR.I.C.K1f	IR.IV.B.K4	IR.VI.B.S17
IR.I.B.K2d	IR.I.C.K1g	IR.IV.B.R4	IR.VI.E.K3
IR.I.B.K2e	IR.I.C.K1h	IR.IV.B.R5	IR.VI.E.R4
IR.I.B.K2f	IR.II.A.K2	IR.IV.B.R6	IR.VII.A.S5
IR.I.B.K2g	IR.II.A.R3	IR.IV.B.R7	IR.VII.B.R6
IR.I.C.K1a	IR.II.A.S2	IR.IV.B.R8	IR.VII.C.S14
IR.I.C.K1b	IR.II.B.K3	IR.IV.B.R9	
IR.I.C.K1c	IR.II.B.S2	IR.IV.B.S2	

- The following ACS codes have been removed and archived. Please see the Airman Certification Standards Companion Guide for Pilots (FAA-G-ACS-2) for more information.

  IR.IV.B.R2
  IR.VII.C.R2

- Non-regulatory material has been moved from the appendices to the Airman Certification Standards Companion Guide for Pilots (FAA-G-ACS-2).

- Legends have been added to the Additional Ratings Task Tables.

Table of Contents

Introduction

Airman Certification Standards Concept

The goal of the airman certification process is to ensure the applicant possesses the knowledge, ability to manage risks, and skill consistent with the privileges of the certificate or rating being exercised, in order to act as pilot-in-command (PIC).

Safe operations in today's National Airspace System (NAS) require the integration of aeronautical knowledge, risk management, and flight proficiency standards. To accomplish these goals, the FAA drew upon the expertise of organizations and individuals across the aviation and training community to develop the ACS. The ACS integrates the elements of knowledge, risk management, and skill required for each airman certificate or rating. It thus forms a more comprehensive standard for what an applicant must know, consider, and do to demonstrate proficiency to pass the tests required for issuance of the applicable airman certificate or rating.

Area of Operation I. Preflight Preparation

Task A. Pilot Qualifications

References: *14 CFR part 61; AC 68-1; FAA-H-8083-2, FAA-H-8083-3, FAA-H-8083-15, FAA-H-8083-25*

Objective: To determine the applicant exhibits satisfactory knowledge, risk management, and skills associated with requirements to act as pilot-in-command under instrument flight rules.

Knowledge:	The applicant demonstrates understanding of:
IR.I.A.K1	Certification requirements, recency of experience, and recordkeeping.
IR.I.A.K2	Privileges and limitations.
IR.I.A.K3	Part 68 BasicMed privileges and limitations.

Risk Management:	The applicant is able to identify, assess, and mitigate risk associated with:
IR.I.A.R1	Proficiency versus currency.
IR.I.A.R2	Personal minimums.
IR.I.A.R3	Fitness for flight and physiological factors that might affect the pilot's ability to fly under instrument conditions.
IR.I.A.R4	Flying unfamiliar aircraft or operating with unfamiliar flight display systems and avionics.

Skills:	The applicant exhibits the skill to:
IR.I.A.S1	Apply requirements to act as pilot-in-command (PIC) under Instrument Flight Rules (IFR) in a scenario given by the evaluator.

Task B. Weather Information

References: *14 CFR part 91, AC 91-92; AIM; FAA-H-8083-2, FAA-H-8083-3, FAA-H-8083-25, FAA-H-8083-28*

Objective: To determine the applicant exhibits satisfactory knowledge, risk management, and skills associated with obtaining, understanding, and applying weather information for a flight under IFR.

Note: *If K2 is selected, the evaluator must assess the applicant's knowledge of at least three sub-elements.*

Note: *If K3 is selected, the evaluator must assess the applicant's knowledge of at least three sub-elements.*

Knowledge:	The applicant demonstrates understanding of:
IR.I.B.K1	Sources of weather data (e.g., National Weather Service, Flight Service) for flight planning purposes.
IR.I.B.K2	Acceptable weather products and resources required for preflight planning, current and forecast weather for departure, en route, and arrival phases of flight such as:
IR.I.B.K2a	a. Airport Observations (METAR and SPECI) and Pilot Observations (PIREP)
IR.I.B.K2b	b. Surface Analysis Chart, Ceiling and Visibility Chart (CVA)
IR.I.B.K2c	c. Terminal Aerodrome Forecasts (TAF)
IR.I.B.K2d	d. Graphical Forecasts for Aviation (GFA)
IR.I.B.K2e	e. Wind and Temperature Aloft Forecast (FB)
IR.I.B.K2f	f. Convective Outlook (AC)

IR.I.B.K2g	g. Inflight Aviation Weather Advisories including Airmen's Meteorological Information (AIRMET), Significant Meteorological Information (SIGMET), and Convective SIGMET
IR.I.B.K3	Meteorology applicable to the departure, en route, alternate, and destination for flights conducted under Instrument Flight Rules (IFR) to include expected climate and hazardous conditions such as:
IR.I.B.K3a	a. Atmospheric composition and stability
IR.I.B.K3b	b. Wind (e.g., windshear, mountain wave, factors affecting wind, etc.)
IR.I.B.K3c	c. Temperature and heat exchange
IR.I.B.K3d	d. Moisture/precipitation
IR.I.B.K3e	e. Weather system formation, including air masses and fronts
IR.I.B.K3f	f. Clouds
IR.I.B.K3g	g. Turbulence
IR.I.B.K3h	h. Thunderstorms and microbursts
IR.I.B.K3i	i. Icing and freezing level information
IR.I.B.K3j	j. Fog/mist
IR.I.B.K3k	k. Frost
IR.I.B.K3l	l. Obstructions to visibility (e.g., smoke, haze, volcanic ash, etc.)
IR.I.B.K4	Flight deck instrument displays of digital weather and aeronautical information.

Risk Management: The applicant is able to identify, assess, and mitigate risk associated with:

IR.I.B.R1	Making the go/no-go and continue/divert decisions, including:
IR.I.B.R1a	a. Circumstances that would make diversion prudent
IR.I.B.R1b	b. Personal weather minimums
IR.I.B.R1c	c. Hazardous weather conditions, including known or forecast icing or turbulence aloft
IR.I.B.R2	Use and limitations of:
IR.I.B.R2a	a. Installed onboard weather equipment
IR.I.B.R2b	b. Aviation weather reports and forecasts
IR.I.B.R2c	c. Inflight weather resources

Skills: The applicant exhibits the skill to:

IR.I.B.S1	Use available aviation weather resources to obtain an adequate weather briefing.
IR.I.B.S2	Analyze the implications of at least three of the conditions listed in K3a through K3l, using actual weather or weather conditions provided by the evaluator.
IR.I.B.S3	Correlate weather information to make a go/no-go decision.
IR.I.B.S4	Determine whether an alternate airport is required, and, if required, whether the selected alternate airport meets regulatory requirements.

Task C. Cross-Country Flight Planning

References: *14 CFR part 91; AIM; Chart Supplements; FAA-H-8083-2, FAA-H-8083-3, FAA-H-8083-15, FAA-H-8083-16, FAA-H-8083-25; IFR Enroute Charts; NOTAMS; IFR Navigation Charts*

Objective: To determine the applicant exhibits satisfactory knowledge, risk management, and skills associated with planning an IFR cross-country and filing an IFR flight plan.

Note: *Preparation, presentation, and explanation of a computer-generated flight plan is an acceptable option.*

Knowledge:	The applicant demonstrates understanding of:
IR.I.C.K1	Route planning, including consideration of:
IR.I.C.K1a	a. Available navigational facilities
IR.I.C.K1b	b. Special use airspace
IR.I.C.K1c	c. Preferred routes
IR.I.C.K1d	d. Primary and alternate airports
IR.I.C.K1e	e. Enroute charts
IR.I.C.K1f	f. Chart Supplements
IR.I.C.K1g	g. NOTAMS
IR.I.C.K1h	h. Terminal Procedures Publications (TPP)
IR.I.C.K2	Altitude selection accounting for terrain and obstacles, glide distance of airplane, IFR cruising altitudes, effect of wind, and oxygen requirements.
IR.I.C.K3	Calculating:
IR.I.C.K3a	a. Time, climb and descent rates, course, distance, heading, true airspeed, and groundspeed
IR.I.C.K3b	b. Estimated time of arrival, including conversion to universal coordinated time (UTC)
IR.I.C.K3c	c. Fuel requirements, including reserve
IR.I.C.K4	Elements of an IFR flight plan.
IR.I.C.K5	Procedures for activating and closing an IFR flight plan in controlled and uncontrolled airspace.

Risk Management:	The applicant is able to identify, assess, and mitigate risk associated with:
IR.I.C.R1	Pilot.
IR.I.C.R2	Aircraft.
IR.I.C.R3	Environment (e.g., weather, airports, airspace, terrain, obstacles).
IR.I.C.R4	External pressures.
IR.I.C.R5	Limitations of air traffic control (ATC) services.
IR.I.C.R6	Limitations of electronic planning applications and programs.
IR.I.C.R7	Fuel planning.

Skills:	The applicant exhibits the skill to:
IR.I.C.S1	Prepare, present, and explain a cross-country flight plan assigned by the evaluator including a risk analysis based on real time weather, which includes calculating time en route and fuel considering factors such as power settings, operating altitude, wind, fuel reserve requirements, and weight and balance requirements.

IR.I.C.S2	Recalculate fuel reserves based on a scenario provided by the evaluator.
IR.I.C.S3	Create a navigation plan and simulate filing an IFR flight plan.
IR.I.C.S4	Interpret departure, arrival, en route, and approach procedures with reference to appropriate and current charts.
IR.I.C.S5	Recognize simulated wing contamination due to airframe icing and demonstrate knowledge of the adverse effects of airframe icing during pre-takeoff, takeoff, cruise, and landing phases of flight as well as the corrective actions.
IR.I.C.S6	Apply pertinent information from appropriate and current aeronautical charts, Chart Supplements; Notices to Air Missions (NOTAMs) relative to airport, runway and taxiway closures; and other flight publications.

Area of Operation II. Preflight Procedures

Task A. Aircraft Systems Related to Instrument Flight Rules (IFR) Operations

References: 14 CFR part 91; AC 91-74; FAA-H-8083-2, FAA-H-8083-3, FAA-H-8083-15, FAA-H-8083-25; POH/AFM

Objective: To determine the applicant exhibits satisfactory knowledge, risk management, and skills associated with anti-icing or deicing systems, and other systems related to IFR flight.

Knowledge:	The applicant demonstrates understanding of:
IR.II.A.K1	The general operational characteristics and limitations of applicable anti-icing and deicing systems, including airframe, propeller, intake, fuel, and pitot-static systems.
IR.II.A.K2	Flight control systems.

Risk Management:	The applicant is able to identify, assess, and mitigate risk associated with:
IR.II.A.R1	Operations in icing conditions.
IR.II.A.R2	Limitations of anti-icing and deicing systems.
IR.II.A.R3	Use of automated systems in instrument conditions.

Skills:	The applicant exhibits the skill to:
IR.II.A.S1	Demonstrate familiarity with anti- or de-icing procedures or information published by the manufacturer specific to the aircraft used on the practical test.
IR.II.A.S2	Demonstrate familiarity with the automatic flight control system (AFCS) procedures or information published by the manufacturer specific to the aircraft used on the practical test, if applicable.

Task B. Aircraft Flight Instruments and Navigation Equipment

References: 14 CFR part 91; AC 90-100, AC 90-105, AC 90-107, AC 91-78, AC 91.21-1; AIM; FAA-H-8083-2, FAA-H-8083-3, FAA-H-8083-15, FAA-H-8083-25

Objective: To determine the applicant exhibits satisfactory knowledge, risk management, and skills associated with managing instruments appropriate for an IFR flight.

Knowledge:	The applicant demonstrates understanding of:
IR.II.B.K1	Operation of the aircraft's applicable flight instrument system(s), including:
IR.II.B.K1a	a. Pitot-static instrument system and associated instruments
IR.II.B.K1b	b. Gyroscopic/electric/vacuum instrument system and associated instruments
IR.II.B.K1c	c. Electrical systems, electronic flight instrument displays [primary flight display (PFD), multi-function display (MFD)], transponder and automatic dependent surveillance–broadcast (ADS-B)
IR.II.B.K1d	d. Magnetic compass
IR.II.B.K2	Operation of the aircraft's applicable navigation system(s), including:
IR.II.B.K2a	a. Very high frequency (VHF) Omnidirectional Range (VOR), distance measuring equipment (DME), instrument landing system (ILS), marker beacon receiver/indicators

| IR.II.B.K2b | b. Area navigation (RNAV), global positioning system (GPS), Wide Area Augmentation System (WAAS), flight management system (FMS), autopilot |
| IR.II.B.K3 | Use of an electronic flight bag (EFB), if used. |

Risk Management: The applicant is able to identify, assess, and mitigate risk associated with:

IR.II.B.R1	Monitoring and management of automated systems.
IR.II.B.R2	Difference between approved and non-approved navigation devices.
IR.II.B.R3	Modes of flight and navigation instruments, including failure conditions.
IR.II.B.R4	Use of an electronic flight bag.
IR.II.B.R5	Use of navigation databases.

Skills: The applicant exhibits the skill to:

| IR.II.B.S1 | Operate and manage installed instruments and navigation equipment. |
| IR.II.B.S2 | Operate and manage an applicant supplied electronic flight bag (EFB), if used. |

Task C. Instrument Flight Deck Check

References: *14 CFR part 91; AC 91.21-1; FAA-H-8083-2, FAA-H-8083-3, FAA-H-8083-15, FAA-H-8083-25; POH/AFM*

Objective: To determine the applicant exhibits satisfactory knowledge, risk management, and skills associated with conducting a preflight check on the aircraft's instruments necessary for an IFR flight.

Knowledge: The applicant demonstrates understanding of:

IR.II.C.K1	Purpose of performing an instrument flight deck check and how to detect possible defects.
IR.II.C.K2	IFR airworthiness, including aircraft inspection requirements and required equipment for IFR flight.
IR.II.C.K3	Required procedures, documentation, and limitations of flying with inoperative equipment.

Risk Management: The applicant is able to identify, assess, and mitigate risk associated with:

| IR.II.C.R1 | Operating with inoperative equipment. |
| IR.II.C.R2 | Operating with outdated navigation publications or databases. |

Skills: The applicant exhibits the skill to:

| IR.II.C.S1 | Perform preflight inspection by following the checklist appropriate to the aircraft and determine if the aircraft is in a condition for safe instrument flight. |

Area of Operation III. Air Traffic Control (ATC) Clearances and Procedures

Task A. Compliance with Air Traffic Control Clearances

References: *14 CFR parts 91; AIM; FAA-H-8083-2, FAA-H-8083-3, FAA-H-8083-15, FAA-H-8083-16, FAA-H-8083-25*

Objective: To determine the applicant exhibits satisfactory knowledge, risk management, and skills associated with ATC clearances and procedures while operating solely by reference to instruments.

Knowledge:	The applicant demonstrates understanding of:
IR.III.A.K1	Elements and procedures related to ATC clearances and pilot/controller responsibilities for departure, en route, and arrival phases of flight, including clearance void times.
IR.III.A.K2	Pilot-in-Command (PIC) emergency authority.
IR.III.A.K3	Lost communication procedures and procedures for flights outside of radar environments.

Risk Management:	The applicant is able to identify, assess, and mitigate risk associated with:
IR.III.A.R1	Less than full understanding of an ATC clearance.
IR.III.A.R2	Inappropriate, incomplete, or incorrect ATC clearances.
IR.III.A.R3	ATC clearance inconsistent with aircraft performance or navigation capability.
IR.III.A.R4	ATC clearance intended for other aircraft with similar call signs.

Skills:	The applicant exhibits the skill to:
IR.III.A.S1	Correctly copy, read back, interpret, and comply with simulated or actual ATC clearances in a timely manner using standard phraseology as provided in the Aeronautical Information Manual (AIM).
IR.III.A.S2	Correctly set communication frequencies, navigation systems (identifying when appropriate), and transponder codes in compliance with the ATC clearance.
IR.III.A.S3	Use the current and appropriate paper or electronic navigation publications.
IR.III.A.S4	Intercept all courses, radials, and bearings appropriate to the procedure, route, or clearance in a timely manner.
IR.III.A.S5	Maintain the applicable airspeed ±10 knots, headings ±10°, altitude ±100 feet; track a course, radial, or bearing within ¾-scale deflection of the course deviation indicator (CDI).
IR.III.A.S6	Use single-pilot resource management (SRM) or crew resource management (CRM), as appropriate.
IR.III.A.S7	Perform the appropriate checklist items relative to the phase of flight.

Task B. Holding Procedures

References: *14 CFR part 91; AIM; FAA-H-8083-2, FAA-H-8083-3, FAA-H-8083-15, FAA-H-8083-16, FAA-H-8083-25*

Objective: To determine the applicant exhibits satisfactory knowledge, risk management, and skills associated with holding procedures solely by reference to instruments.

Knowledge:	The applicant demonstrates understanding of:
IR.III.B.K1	Elements related to holding procedures, including reporting criteria, appropriate speeds, and recommended entry procedures for standard, nonstandard, published, and non-published holding patterns.

Risk Management:	The applicant is able to identify, assess, and mitigate risk associated with:
IR.III.B.R1	Recalculating fuel reserves if assigned an unanticipated expect further clearance (EFC) time.
IR.III.B.R2	Scenarios and circumstances that could result in minimum fuel or the need to declare an emergency.
IR.III.B.R3	Scenarios that could lead to holding, including deteriorating weather at the planned destination.
IR.III.B.R4	Holding entry and wind correction while holding.

Skills:	The applicant exhibits the skill to:
IR.III.B.S1	Use an entry procedure appropriate for a standard, nonstandard, published, or non-published holding pattern.
IR.III.B.S2	Change to the holding airspeed appropriate for the altitude when 3 minutes or less from, but prior to arriving at, the holding fix and set appropriate power as needed for fuel conservation.
IR.III.B.S3	Recognize arrival at the holding fix and promptly initiate entry into the holding pattern.
IR.III.B.S3a	a. Comply with the holding pattern leg length and other restrictions, if applicable, associated with the holding pattern
IR.III.B.S4	Maintain airspeed ±10 knots, altitude ±100 feet, selected headings within ±10°, and track a selected course, radial, or bearing within ¾-scale deflection of the course deviation indicator (CDI).
IR.III.B.S5	Use proper wind correction procedures to maintain the desired pattern and to arrive over the fix as close as possible to a specified time.
IR.III.B.S6	Use a multi-function display (MFD) and other graphical navigation displays, if installed, to monitor position in relation to the desired flightpath during holding.
IR.III.B.S7	Comply with ATC reporting requirements and restrictions associated with the holding pattern.
IR.III.B.S8	Use single-pilot resource management (SRM) or crew resource management (CRM), as appropriate.

Area of Operation IV. Flight by Reference to Instruments

Task A. Instrument Flight

References: FAA-H-8083-2, FAA-H-8083-3, FAA-H-8083-15, FAA-H-8083-16, FAA-H-8083-25

Objective: To determine the applicant exhibits satisfactory knowledge, risk management, and skills associated with performing basic flight maneuvers solely by reference to instruments.

Knowledge:	The applicant demonstrates understanding of:
IR.IV.A.K1	Elements related to attitude instrument flying during straight-and-level flight, climbs, turns, and descents while conducting various instrument flight procedures.
IR.IV.A.K2	Interpretation, operation, and limitations of pitch, bank, and power instruments.
IR.IV.A.K3	Normal and abnormal instrument indications and operations.

Risk Management:	The applicant is able to identify, assess, and mitigate risk associated with:
IR.IV.A.R1	Situations that can affect physiology and degrade instrument cross-check.
IR.IV.A.R2	Spatial disorientation and optical illusions.
IR.IV.A.R3	Flying unfamiliar aircraft or operating with unfamiliar flight display systems and avionics.

Skills:	The applicant exhibits the skill to:
IR.IV.A.S1	Maintain altitude ±100 feet during level flight, selected headings ±10°, airspeed ±10 knots, and bank angles ±5° during turns.
IR.IV.A.S2	Use proper instrument cross-check and interpretation, and apply the appropriate pitch, bank, power, and trim corrections when applicable.

Task B. Recovery from Unusual Flight Attitudes

References: FAA-H-8083-2, FAA-H-8083-3, FAA-H-8083-15, FAA-H-8083-25; POH/AFM

Objective: To determine the applicant exhibits satisfactory knowledge, risk management, and skills associated with recovering from unusual flight attitudes solely by reference to instruments.

Knowledge:	The applicant demonstrates understanding of:
IR.IV.B.K1	Procedures for recovery from unusual attitudes in flight.
IR.IV.B.K2	Prevention of unusual attitudes, including flight causal, physiological, and environmental factors, and system and equipment failures.
IR.IV.B.K3	Procedures available to safely regain visual meteorological conditions (VMC) after flight into inadvertent instrument meteorological conditions or unintended instrument meteorological conditions (IIMC)/(UIMC).
IR.IV.B.K4	Appropriate use of automation, if applicable.

Risk Management:	The applicant is able to identify, assess, and mitigate risk associated with:
IR.IV.B.R1	Situations that could lead to loss of control in-flight (LOC-I) or unusual attitudes in-flight (e.g., stress, task saturation, inadequate instrument scan distractions, and spatial disorientation).
IR.IV.B.R2	[Archived]

IR.IV.B.R3	Operating envelope considerations.
IR.IV.B.R4	Interpreting flight instruments.
IR.IV.B.R5	Assessment of the unusual attitude.
IR.IV.B.R6	Control input errors, inducing undesired aircraft attitudes.
IR.IV.B.R7	Control application solely by reference to instruments.
IR.IV.B.R8	Collision hazards.
IR.IV.B.R9	Distractions, task prioritization, loss of situational awareness, or disorientation.

Skills:	The applicant exhibits the skill to:
IR.IV.B.S1	Use proper instrument cross-check and interpretation to identify an unusual attitude (including both nose-high and nose-low) in flight, and apply the appropriate flight control, power input, and aircraft configuration in the correct sequence, to return to a stabilized level flight attitude.
IR.IV.B.S2	Use single-pilot resource management (SRM) or crew resource management (CRM), as appropriate.

Area of Operation V. Navigation Systems

Task A. Intercepting and Tracking Navigational Systems and DME Arcs

References: *14 CFR part 91; AIM; FAA-H-8083-2, FAA-H-8083-3, FAA-H-8083-15, FAA-H-8083-16, FAA-H-8083-25; POH/AFM*

Objective: To determine the applicant exhibits satisfactory knowledge, risk management, and skills associated with intercepting and tracking navigation aids and arcs solely by reference to instruments.

Note: *The evaluator should reference the manufacturer's equipment supplement(s) as necessary for appropriate limitations, procedures, etc.*

Note: *See Appendix 3: Aircraft, Equipment, and Operational Requirements & Limitations for information related to this Task.*

Knowledge:	The applicant demonstrates understanding of:
IR.V.A.K1	Ground-based navigation (orientation, course determination, equipment, tests, and regulations), including procedures for intercepting and tracking courses and arcs.
IR.V.A.K2	Satellite-based navigation (orientation, course determination, equipment, tests, regulations, interference, appropriate use of databases, Receiver Autonomous Integrity Monitoring (RAIM), and Wide Area Augmentation System (WAAS)), including procedures for intercepting and tracking courses and arcs.

Risk Management:	The applicant is able to identify, assess, and mitigate risk associated with:
IR.V.A.R1	Management of automated navigation and autoflight systems.
IR.V.A.R2	Distractions, task prioritization, loss of situational awareness, or disorientation.
IR.V.A.R3	Limitations of the navigation system in use.

Skills:	The applicant exhibits the skill to:
IR.V.A.S1	Tune and identify the navigation facility/program the navigation system and verify system accuracy as appropriate for the equipment installed in the aircraft.
IR.V.A.S2	Determine aircraft position relative to the navigational facility or waypoint.
IR.V.A.S3	Set and orient to the course to be intercepted.
IR.V.A.S4	Intercept the specified course at appropriate angle, inbound to or outbound from a navigational facility or waypoint.
IR.V.A.S5	Maintain airspeed ±10 knots, altitude ±100 feet, and selected headings ±5°.
IR.V.A.S6	Apply proper correction to maintain a course, allowing no more than ¾-scale deflection of the course deviation indicator (CDI). If a distance measuring equipment (DME) arc is selected, maintain that arc ±1 nautical mile.
IR.V.A.S7	Recognize navigational system or facility failure, and when required, report the failure to air traffic control (ATC).
IR.V.A.S8	Use a multi-function display (MFD) and other graphical navigation displays, if installed, to monitor position, track wind drift, and to maintain situational awareness.
IR.V.A.S9	At the discretion of the evaluator, use the autopilot to make appropriate course intercepts, if installed.
IR.V.A.S10	Use single-pilot resource management (SRM) or crew resource management (CRM), as appropriate.

Task B. Departure, En Route, and Arrival Operations

References: *14 CFR parts 91, 97; AC 90-100, AC 90-105, AC 91-74; AIM; FAA-H-8083-2, FAA-H-8083-3, FAA-H-8083-15, FAA-H-8083-16, FAA-H-8083-25; POH/AFM*

Objective: To determine the applicant exhibits satisfactory knowledge, risk management, and skills associated with IFR departure, en route, and arrival operations solely by reference to instruments.

Knowledge:	The applicant demonstrates understanding of:
IR.V.B.K1	Elements related to ATC routes, including departure procedures (DPs) and associated climb gradients; standard terminal arrival (STAR) procedures and associated constraints.
IR.V.B.K2	Pilot/controller responsibilities, communication procedures, and ATC services available to pilots.

Risk Management:	The applicant is able to identify, assess, and mitigate risk associated with:
IR.V.B.R1	ATC communications and compliance with published procedures.
IR.V.B.R2	Limitations of traffic avoidance equipment.
IR.V.B.R3	Responsibility to use "see and avoid" techniques when possible.

Skills:	The applicant exhibits the skill to:
IR.V.B.S1	Select, identify (as necessary) and use the appropriate communication and navigation facilities associated with the proposed flight.
IR.V.B.S2	Perform the appropriate checklist items relative to the phase of flight.
IR.V.B.S3	Use the current and appropriate paper or electronic navigation publications.
IR.V.B.S4	Establish two-way communications with the proper controlling agency, use proper phraseology, and comply in a timely manner with all ATC instructions and airspace restrictions.
IR.V.B.S5	Intercept all courses, radials, and bearings appropriate to the procedure, route, or clearance in a timely manner.
IR.V.B.S6	Comply with all applicable charted procedures.
IR.V.B.S7	Maintain airspeed ±10 knots, altitude ±100 feet, and selected headings ±10°, and apply proper correction to maintain a course allowing no more than ¾-scale deflection of the course deviation indicator (CDI).
IR.V.B.S8	Update/interpret weather in flight.
IR.V.B.S9	Use displays of digital weather and aeronautical information, as applicable to maintain situational awareness.
IR.V.B.S10	Use single-pilot resource management (SRM) or crew resource management (CRM), as appropriate.

Area of Operation VI. Instrument Approach Procedures

Task A. Non-precision Approach

References: *14 CFR part 91; AC 120-108; AIM; FAA-H-8083-2, FAA-H-8083-3, FAA-H-8083-15, FAA-H-8083-16, FAA-H-8083-25; Terminal Procedures Publications*

Objective: To determine the applicant exhibits satisfactory knowledge, risk management, and skills associated with performing non-precision approach procedures solely by reference to instruments.

Note: *See Appendix 3: Aircraft, Equipment, and Operational Requirements & Limitations for information related to this Task.*

Knowledge:	The applicant demonstrates understanding of:
IR.VI.A.K1	Procedures and limitations associated with a non-precision approach, including the differences between Localizer Performance (LP) and Lateral Navigation (LNAV) approach guidance.
IR.VI.A.K2	Navigation system indications and annunciations expected during an area navigation (RNAV) approach.
IR.VI.A.K3	Ground-based and satellite-based navigation systems used for a non-precision approach.
IR.VI.A.K4	A stabilized approach, including energy management concepts.

Risk Management:	The applicant is able to identify, assess, and mitigate risk associated with:
IR.VI.A.R1	Deviating from the assigned approach procedure.
IR.VI.A.R2	Selecting a navigation frequency.
IR.VI.A.R3	Management of automated navigation and autoflight systems.
IR.VI.A.R4	Aircraft configuration during an approach and missed approach.
IR.VI.A.R5	An unstable approach, including excessive descent rates.
IR.VI.A.R6	Deteriorating weather conditions on approach.
IR.VI.A.R7	Operating below the minimum descent altitude (MDA) without proper visual references.

Skills:	The applicant exhibits the skill to:
IR.VI.A.S1	Accomplish the non-precision instrument approaches selected by the evaluator.
IR.VI.A.S2	Establish two-way communications with air traffic control (ATC) appropriate for the phase of flight or approach segment, and use proper communication phraseology.
IR.VI.A.S3	Select, tune, identify, and confirm the operational status of navigation equipment to be used for the approach.
IR.VI.A.S4	Comply with all clearances issued by ATC or the evaluator.
IR.VI.A.S5	Recognize if any flight instrumentation is inaccurate or inoperative, and take appropriate action.
IR.VI.A.S6	Advise ATC or the evaluator if unable to comply with a clearance.
IR.VI.A.S7	Complete the appropriate checklist(s).
IR.VI.A.S8	Establish the appropriate aircraft configuration and airspeed considering meteorological and operating conditions.

IR.VI.A.S9	Maintain altitude ±100 feet, selected heading ±10°, airspeed ±10 knots, no more than ¾ scale CDI deflection, and accurately track radials, courses, or bearings, prior to beginning the final approach segment.
IR.VI.A.S10	Adjust the published MDA and visibility criteria for the aircraft approach category, as appropriate, for factors that include Notices of Air Missions (NOTAMs), inoperative aircraft or navigation equipment, or inoperative visual aids associated with the landing environment, etc.
IR.VI.A.S11	Establish a stabilized descent to the appropriate altitude.
IR.VI.A.S12	For the final approach segment, maintain no more than ¾ scale CDI deflection, airspeed ±10 knots, and altitude, if applicable, above MDA +100/-0 feet to the Visual Descent Point (VDP) or missed approach point (MAP).
IR.VI.A.S13	Assess if the required visual references are available, and either initiate the missed approach procedure or continue for landing.
IR.VI.A.S14	Use a multi-function display (MFD) and other graphical navigation displays, if installed, to monitor position, track wind drift, and to maintain situational awareness.
IR.VI.A.S15	Use single-pilot resource management (SRM) or crew resource management (CRM), as appropriate.

Task B. Precision Approach

References: *14 CFR part 91; AC 90-105, AC 90-107; AIM; FAA-H-8083-2, FAA-H-8083-3, FAA-H-8083-15, FAA-H-8083-16, FAA-H-8083-25; Terminal Procedures Publications*

Objective: To determine the applicant exhibits satisfactory knowledge, risk management, and skills associated with performing precision approach procedures solely by reference to instruments.

Note: *See Appendix 3: Aircraft, Equipment, and Operational Requirements & Limitations for information related to this Task.*

Knowledge: The applicant demonstrates understanding of:

IR.VI.B.K1	Procedures and limitations associated with a precision approach, including determining required descent rates and adjusting minimums in the case of inoperative equipment.
IR.VI.B.K2	Navigation system displays, annunciations, and modes of operation.
IR.VI.B.K3	Ground-based and satellite-based navigation systems (orientation, course determination, equipment, tests and regulations, interference, appropriate use of navigation data, signal integrity).
IR.VI.B.K4	A stabilized approach, including energy management concepts.

Risk Management: The applicant is able to identify, assess, and mitigate risk associated with:

IR.VI.B.R1	Deviating from the assigned approach procedure.
IR.VI.B.R2	Selecting a navigation frequency.
IR.VI.B.R3	Management of automated navigation and autoflight systems.
IR.VI.B.R4	Aircraft configuration during an approach and missed approach.
IR.VI.B.R5	An unstable approach, including excessive descent rates.
IR.VI.B.R6	Deteriorating weather conditions on approach.
IR.VI.B.R7	Continuing to descend below the Decision Altitude (DA)/Decision Height (DH) when the required visual references are not visible.

Skills: The applicant exhibits the skill to:

IR.VI.B.S1	Accomplish the precision instrument approach(es) selected by the evaluator.
IR.VI.B.S2	Establish two-way communications with air traffic control (ATC) appropriate for the phase of flight or approach segment, and use proper communication phraseology.
IR.VI.B.S3	Select, tune, identify, and confirm the operational status of navigation equipment to be used for the approach.
IR.VI.B.S4	Comply with all clearances issued by ATC or the evaluator.
IR.VI.B.S5	Recognize if any flight instrumentation is inaccurate or inoperative, and take appropriate action.
IR.VI.B.S6	Advise ATC or the evaluator if unable to comply with a clearance.
IR.VI.B.S7	Complete the appropriate checklist(s).
IR.VI.B.S8	Establish the appropriate aircraft configuration and airspeed considering meteorological and operating conditions.
IR.VI.B.S9	Maintain altitude ±100 feet, selected heading ±10°, airspeed ±10 knots, no more than ¾ scale CDI deflection, and accurately track radials, courses, or bearings, prior to beginning the final approach segment.
IR.VI.B.S10	Adjust the published DA/DH and visibility criteria for the aircraft approach category, as appropriate, to account for NOTAMS, inoperative aircraft or navigation equipment, or inoperative visual aids associated with the landing environment.
IR.VI.B.S11	Establish a predetermined rate of descent at the point where vertical guidance begins, which approximates that required for the aircraft to follow the vertical guidance.
IR.VI.B.S12	Maintain a stabilized final approach from the final approach fix (FAF) to DA/DH allowing no more than ¾-scale deflection of either the vertical or lateral guidance indications, and maintain the desired airspeed ±10 knots.
IR.VI.B.S13	Immediately initiate the missed approach procedure when at the DA/DH, and the required visual references for the runway are not unmistakably visible and identifiable.
IR.VI.B.S14	Transition to a normal landing approach (missed approach for seaplanes) only when the airplane is in a position from which a descent to a landing on the runway can be made at a normal rate of descent using normal maneuvering.
IR.VI.B.S15	Maintain a stabilized visual flight path from the DA/DH to the runway aiming point where a normal landing may be accomplished within the touchdown zone.
IR.VI.B.S16	Use a multi-function display (MFD) and other graphical navigation displays, if installed, to monitor position, track wind drift, and to maintain situational awareness.
IR.VI.B.S17	Use single-pilot resource management (SRM) or crew resource management (CRM), as appropriate.

Task C. Missed Approach

References: 14 CFR parts 91, 97; AIM; FAA-H-8083-2, FAA-H-8083-3, FAA-H-8083-15, FAA-H-8083-16, FAA-H-8083-25; Terminal Procedures Publications

Objective: To determine the applicant exhibits satisfactory knowledge, risk management, and skills associated with performing a missed approach procedure solely by reference to instruments.

Knowledge: The applicant demonstrates understanding of:

IR.VI.C.K1	Elements related to missed approach procedures and limitations associated with standard instrument approaches, including while using a flight management system (FMS) or autopilot, if equipped.

Risk

Management: The applicant is able to identify, assess, and mitigate risk associated with:

IR.VI.C.R1	Deviations from prescribed procedures or ATC instructions.
IR.VI.C.R2	Holding, diverting, or electing to fly the approach again.
IR.VI.C.R3	Aircraft configuration during an approach and missed approach.
IR.VI.C.R4	Factors that might lead to executing a missed approach procedure before the MAP or to a go-around below DA, DH, or MDA, as applicable.
IR.VI.C.R5	Management of automated navigation and autoflight systems.

Skills: The applicant exhibits the skill to:

IR.VI.C.S1	Promptly initiate the missed approach procedure and report it to ATC.
IR.VI.C.S2	Apply the appropriate power setting for the flight condition and establish a pitch attitude necessary to obtain the desired performance.
IR.VI.C.S3	Configure the airplane in accordance with airplane manufacturer's instructions, establish a positive rate of climb, and accelerate to the appropriate airspeed, ±10 knots.
IR.VI.C.S4	Follow the recommended checklist items appropriate to the missed approach/go-around procedure.
IR.VI.C.S5	Comply with the published or alternate missed approach procedure.
IR.VI.C.S6	Advise ATC or the evaluator if unable to comply with a clearance, restriction, or climb gradient.
IR.VI.C.S7	Maintain the recommended airspeed ±10 knots; heading, course, or bearing ±10°; and altitude(s) ±100 feet during the missed approach procedure.
IR.VI.C.S8	Use an MFD and other graphical navigation displays, if installed, to monitor position and track to help navigate the missed approach.
IR.VI.C.S9	Use single-pilot resource management (SRM) or crew resource management (CRM), as appropriate.
IR.VI.C.S10	Request ATC clearance to attempt another approach, proceed to the alternate airport, holding fix, or other clearance limit, as appropriate, or as directed by the evaluator.

Task D. Circling Approach

References: *14 CFR parts 91, 97; AIM; FAA-H-8083-2, FAA-H-8083-3, FAA-H-8083-15, FAA-H-8083-16, FAA-H-8083-25; Terminal Procedures Publications*

Objective: To determine the applicant exhibits satisfactory knowledge, risk management, and skills associated with performing a circling approach procedure.

Knowledge: The applicant demonstrates understanding of:

IR.VI.D.K1	Elements related to circling approach procedures and limitations, including approach categories and related airspeed restrictions.

Risk

Management: The applicant is able to identify, assess, and mitigate risk associated with:

IR.VI.D.R1	Prescribed circling approach procedures.
IR.VI.D.R2	Executing a circling approach at night or with marginal visibility.
IR.VI.D.R3	Losing visual contact with an identifiable part of the airport.

IR.VI.D.R4	Management of automated navigation and autoflight systems.
IR.VI.D.R5	Management of altitude, airspeed, or distance while circling.
IR.VI.D.R6	Low altitude maneuvering, including stall, spin, or controlled flight into terrain (CFIT).
IR.VI.D.R7	Executing a missed approach after the MAP while circling.

Skills:	The applicant exhibits the skill to:
IR.VI.D.S1	Comply with the circling approach procedure considering turbulence, windshear, and the maneuvering capability and approach category of the aircraft.
IR.VI.D.S2	Confirm the direction of traffic and adhere to all restrictions and instructions issued by ATC or the evaluator.
IR.VI.D.S3	Use single-pilot resource management (SRM) or crew resource management (CRM), as appropriate.
IR.VI.D.S4	Establish the approach and landing configuration. Maintain a stabilized approach and a descent rate that ensures arrival at the MDA, or the preselected circling altitude above the MDA, prior to the missed approach point.
IR.VI.D.S5	Maintain airspeed ±10 knots, desired heading/track ±10°, and altitude +100/-0 feet until descending below the MDA or the preselected circling altitude above the MDA.
IR.VI.D.S6	Visually maneuver to a base or downwind leg appropriate for the landing runway and environmental conditions.
IR.VI.D.S7	If a missed approach occurs, turn in the appropriate direction using the correct procedure and appropriately configure the airplane.
IR.VI.D.S8	If landing, initiate a stabilized descent. Touch down on the first one-third of the selected runway without excessive maneuvering, without exceeding the normal operating limits of the airplane, and without exceeding 30° of bank.

Task E. Landing from an Instrument Approach

References: *14 CFR parts 91; AIM; FAA-H-8083-2, FAA-H-8083-3, FAA-H-8083-15, FAA-H-8083-16, FAA-H-8083-25; POH/AFM*

Objective: To determine the applicant exhibits satisfactory knowledge, risk management, and skills associated with performing procedures for a landing from an instrument approach.

Note: *For non-amphibious seaplanes, this task applies only when the applicant has immediate access to an instrument approach to a waterway.*

Knowledge:	The applicant demonstrates understanding of:
IR.VI.E.K1	Elements related to the pilot's responsibilities, and the environmental, operational, and meteorological factors that affect landing from a straight-in or circling approach.
IR.VI.E.K2	Airport signs, markings, and lighting, including approach lighting systems.
IR.VI.E.K3	Appropriate landing profiles and aircraft configurations.

Risk Management:	The applicant is able to identify, assess, and mitigate risk associated with:
IR.VI.E.R1	Attempting to land from an unstable approach.
IR.VI.E.R2	Flying below the glidepath.

Instrument Rating – Airplane ACS (FAA-S-ACS-8C)

| IR.VI.E.R3 | Transitioning from instrument to visual references for landing. |
| IR.VI.E.R4 | Aircraft configuration for landing. |

Skills:	The applicant exhibits the skill to:
IR.VI.E.S1	Transition at the DA/DH, MDA, or visual descent point (VDP) to a visual flight condition, allowing for safe visual maneuvering and a normal landing.
IR.VI.E.S2	Adhere to all ATC or evaluator advisories, such as NOTAMs, windshear, wake turbulence, runway surface, and other operational considerations.
IR.VI.E.S3	Complete the appropriate checklist(s).
IR.VI.E.S4	Maintain positive airplane control throughout the landing maneuver.
IR.VI.E.S5	Use single-pilot resource management (SRM) or crew resource management (CRM), as appropriate.

Area of Operation VII. Emergency Operations

Task A. Loss of Communications

References: *14 CFR part 91; AIM; FAA-H-8083-2, FAA-H-8083-3, FAA-H-8083-15, FAA-H-8083-16, FAA-H-8083-25*

Objective: To determine the applicant exhibits satisfactory knowledge, risk management, and skills associated with loss of communications while operating solely by reference to instruments.

Knowledge:	The applicant demonstrates understanding of:
IR.VII.A.K1	Procedures to follow in the event of lost communication during various phases of flight, including techniques for reestablishing communications, when it is acceptable to deviate from an instrument flight rules (IFR) clearance, and when to begin an approach at the destination.

Risk Management:	The applicant is able to identify, assess, and mitigate risk associated with:
IR.VII.A.R1	Possible reasons for loss of communication.
IR.VII.A.R2	Deviation from procedures for lost communications.

Skills:	The applicant exhibits the skill to:
IR.VII.A.S1	Recognize a simulated loss of communication.
IR.VII.A.S2	Simulate actions to re-establish communication.
IR.VII.A.S3	Determine whether to continue to flight plan destination or deviate.
IR.VII.A.S4	Determine appropriate time to begin an approach.
IR.VII.A.S5	Use single-pilot resource management (SRM) or crew resource management (CRM), as appropriate.

Task B. One Engine Inoperative (Simulated) during Straight-and-Level Flight and Turns (AMEL, AMES)

References: *FAA-H-8083-2, FAA-H-8083-3, FAA-H-8083-15, FAA-H-8083-25; POH/AFM*

Objective: To determine the applicant exhibits satisfactory knowledge, risk management, and skills associated with flight solely by reference to instruments with one engine inoperative.

Note: *See Appendix 2: Safety of Flight.*

Knowledge:	The applicant demonstrates understanding of:
IR.VII.B.K1	Procedures used if engine failure occurs during straight-and-level flight and turns while on instruments.

Risk Management:	The applicant is able to identify, assess, and mitigate risk associated with:
IR.VII.B.R1	Identification of the inoperative engine.
IR.VII.B.R2	Inability to climb or maintain altitude with an inoperative engine.
IR.VII.B.R3	Low altitude maneuvering, including stall, spin, or controlled flight into terrain (CFIT).
IR.VII.B.R4	Distractions, task prioritization, loss of situational awareness, or disorientation.

| IR.VII.B.R5 | Fuel management during single-engine operation. |
| IR.VII.B.R6 | Configuring the aircraft. |

Skills: The applicant exhibits the skill to:

IR.VII.B.S1	Promptly recognize an engine failure and maintain positive aircraft control.
IR.VII.B.S2	Set the engine controls, reduce drag, identify and verify the inoperative engine, and simulate feathering of the propeller on the inoperative engine (evaluator should then establish zero thrust on the inoperative engine).
IR.VII.B.S3	Establish the best engine-inoperative airspeed and trim the airplane.
IR.VII.B.S4	Use flight controls in the proper combination as recommended by the manufacturer, or as required to maintain best performance, and trim as required.
IR.VII.B.S5	Verify the prescribed checklist procedures used for securing the inoperative engine.
IR.VII.B.S6	Attempt to determine and resolve the reason for the engine failure.
IR.VII.B.S7	Monitor engine functions and make necessary adjustments.
IR.VII.B.S8	Maintain the specified altitude ±100 feet or minimum sink rate if applicable, airspeed ±10 knots, and the specified heading ±10°.
IR.VII.B.S9	Assess the aircraft's performance capability and decide an appropriate action to ensure a safe landing.
IR.VII.B.S10	Maintain control and fly within the aircraft's operating limitations.
IR.VII.B.S11	Use single-pilot resource management (SRM) or crew resource management (CRM), as appropriate.

Task C. Instrument Approach and Landing with an Inoperative Engine (Simulated) (AMEL, AMES)

References: 14 CFR part 91; FAA-H-8083-2, FAA-H-8083-3, FAA-H-8083-15, FAA-H-8083-16, FAA-H-8083-25; POH/AFM; Terminal Procedures Publications

Objective: To determine the applicant exhibits satisfactory knowledge, risk management, and skills associated with executing a published instrument approach solely by reference to instruments with one engine inoperative.

Note: See Appendix 2: Safety of Flight and Appendix 3: Aircraft, Equipment, and Operational Requirements & Limitations for information related to this Task.

Note: For non-amphibious seaplanes, this task applies only when the applicant has immediate access to an instrument approach to a waterway.

Knowledge: The applicant demonstrates understanding of:

| IR.VII.C.K1 | Instrument approach procedures with one engine inoperative. |

Risk Management: The applicant is able to identify, assess, and mitigate risk associated with:

IR.VII.C.R1	Potential engine failure during approach and landing.
IR.VII.C.R2	[Archived]
IR.VII.C.R3	Configuring the airplane.
IR.VII.C.R4	Low altitude maneuvering, including stall, spin, or controlled flight into terrain (CFIT).

IR.VII.C.R5	Distractions, task prioritization, loss of situational awareness, or disorientation.
IR.VII.C.R6	Performing a go-around/rejected landing with an engine failure.

Skills:	The applicant exhibits the skill to:
IR.VII.C.S1	Promptly recognize an engine failure and maintain positive aircraft control.
IR.VII.C.S2	Set the engine controls, reduce drag, identify and verify the inoperative engine, and simulate feathering of the propeller on the inoperative engine (evaluator should then establish zero thrust on the inoperative engine).
IR.VII.C.S3	Use flight controls in the proper combination as recommended by the manufacturer, or as required to maintain best performance, and trim as required.
IR.VII.C.S4	Follow the manufacturer's recommended emergency procedures and complete the appropriate checklist.
IR.VII.C.S5	Monitor the operating engine and aircraft systems and make adjustments as necessary.
IR.VII.C.S6	Request and follow an actual or a simulated air traffic control (ATC) clearance for an instrument approach.
IR.VII.C.S7	Maintain altitude ±100 feet or minimum sink rate if applicable, airspeed ±10 knots, and selected heading ±10°.
IR.VII.C.S8	Establish a rate of descent that ensures arrival at the minimum descent altitude (MDA) or decision altitude (DA)/decision height (DH) with the airplane in a position from which a descent to a landing on the intended runway can be made, either straight in or circling as appropriate.
IR.VII.C.S9	On final approach segment, maintain vertical (as applicable) and lateral guidance within ¾-scale deflection.
IR.VII.C.S10	Maintain control and fly within the aircraft's operating limitations.
IR.VII.C.S11	Comply with the published criteria for the aircraft approach category if circling.
IR.VII.C.S12	Execute a landing.
IR.VII.C.S13	Complete the appropriate checklist(s).
IR.VII.C.S14	Use single-pilot resource management (SRM) or crew resource management (CRM), as appropriate.

Task D. Approach with Loss of Primary Flight Instrument Indicators

References:	14 CFR part 91; FAA-H-8083-2, FAA-H-8083-3, FAA-H-8083-15, FAA-H-8083-16, FAA-H-8083-25; POH/AFM; Terminal Procedures Publications
Objective:	To determine the applicant exhibits satisfactory knowledge, risk management, and skills associated with performing an approach solely by reference to instruments with the loss of primary flight control instruments.

Knowledge:	The applicant demonstrates understanding of:
IR.VII.D.K1	Recognizing if primary flight instruments are inaccurate or inoperative, and advising ATC or the evaluator.
IR.VII.D.K2	Possible failure modes of primary instruments and how to correct or minimize the effect of the loss.

Risk
Management: The applicant is able to identify, assess, and mitigate risk associated with:

IR.VII.D.R1	Use of secondary flight displays when primary displays have failed.
IR.VII.D.R2	Maintaining aircraft control.
IR.VII.D.R3	Distractions, task prioritization, loss of situational awareness, or disorientation.

Skills: The applicant exhibits the skill to:

IR.VII.D.S1	Advise ATC or the evaluator if unable to comply with a clearance.
IR.VII.D.S2	Complete a non-precision instrument approach without the use of the primary flight instruments using the skill elements of the non-precision approach Task (see Area of Operation VI, Task A).
IR.VII.D.S3	Use single-pilot resource management (SRM) or crew resource management (CRM), as appropriate.

Area of Operation VIII. Postflight Procedures

Task A. Checking Instruments and Equipment

References: *14 CFR part 91; FAA-H-8083-2, FAA-H-8083-3, FAA-H-8083-25; POH/AFM*

Objective: To determine the applicant exhibits satisfactory knowledge, risk management, and skills associated with checking flight instruments and equipment during postflight.

Knowledge:	The applicant demonstrates understanding of:
IR.VIII.A.K1	Procedures for documenting in-flight/postflight discrepancies.

Risk Management:	The applicant is able to identify, assess, and mitigate risk associated with:
IR.VIII.A.R1	Performance and documentation of postflight inspection and aircraft discrepancies.

Skills:	The applicant exhibits the skill to:
IR.VIII.A.S1	Conduct a postflight inspection and document discrepancies and servicing requirements, if any.

Appendix 1: Practical Test Roles, Responsibilities, and Outcomes

Eligibility Requirements for an Instrument Rating

The prerequisite requirements and general eligibility for a practical test and the specific requirements for the issuance of an Instrument Rating – Airplane can be found in 14 CFR part 61, sections 61.39(a) and 61.65.

If an applicant holds both single-engine and multiengine class ratings on a pilot certificate and takes the instrument rating practical test in a single-engine airplane, the certificate issued must bear the limitation "Multiengine Limited to VFR Only." If the applicant takes the test in a multiengine airplane, the instrument privileges will be automatically conferred for the airplane single-engine rating.

In accordance with 14 CFR part 61, sections 61.39, and 61.65(a)(7), the applicant must pass the airman knowledge test before taking the practical test, if applicable to the certificate or rating sought. Applicants who hold an instrument rating are not required to take an additional instrument knowledge test.

The knowledge test corresponding to this ACS appears in the table below.

Test Code	Test Name	Number of Questions	Age	Allotted Time	Passing Score
IRA	Instrument Rating – Airplane	60	15	2.5	70

Use of the ACS During a Practical Test

The practical test is conducted in accordance with the ACS and FAA regulations that are current as of the date of the test.

The Areas of Operation in this ACS align with the Areas of Operation found in 14 CFR part 61, section 61.65(c). Each Area of Operation includes Tasks appropriate to that Area of Operation. Each Task contains an Objective stating what the applicant must know, consider, and/or do. The ACS then lists the aeronautical knowledge, risk management, and skill elements relevant to the specific Task, along with the conditions and standards for acceptable performance. The ACS uses Notes to emphasize special considerations.

During the ground and flight portion of the practical test, the FAA expects evaluators to assess the applicant's mastery of the topic in accordance with the level of learning most appropriate for the specified Task. The oral questioning will continue throughout the entire practical test. For some topics, the evaluator will ask the applicant to describe or explain. For other items, the evaluator will assess the applicant's understanding by providing a scenario that requires the applicant to appropriately apply and/or correlate knowledge, experience, and information to the circumstances of the given scenario. The flight portion of the practical test requires the applicant to demonstrate knowledge, risk management, flight proficiency, and operational skill in accordance with the ACS.

The elements within each Task in this ACS are coded according to a scheme that includes four components. For example, IR.I.B.K4:

> IR = Applicable
>
> ACS I = Area of Operation
>
> B =Task
>
> K4 = Task element (in this example, Knowledge 4)

There is no requirement for an evaluator to test every knowledge and risk management element in a Task; rather the evaluator has discretion to sample as needed to ensure the applicant's mastery of that Task. The required minimum elements to be tested from each applicable Task include:

- any elements in which the applicant was shown to be deficient on the knowledge test, as applicable;
- at least one knowledge element;
- at least one risk management element; and
- all skill elements unless otherwise noted.

The Airman Knowledge Test Report (AKTR) lists ACS codes that correlate to a specific Task element for a given Area of Operation for any incorrect responses on the knowledge test.

Knowledge and risk management elements are primarily evaluated during the knowledge testing phase of the airman certification process. The evaluator administering the practical test has the discretion to combine Tasks/elements as appropriate to testing scenarios.

Unless otherwise noted in the Task, the evaluator must test each item in the skills section by observing the applicant perform each one. As safety of flight conditions permit, the evaluator should use questions during flight to test knowledge and risk management elements not evident in the demonstrated skills. To the greatest extent practicable, evaluators should test the applicant's ability to apply and correlate information and use rote questions only when they are appropriate for the material being tested.

If the Task includes a knowledge or risk element with sub-elements, the evaluator may choose the primary element and select at least one sub-element to satisfy the requirement. Selection of the sub-element satisfies the requirement for one element unless otherwise noted.

For example, an evaluator who chooses IR.I.B.K3 may select a sub-element such as IR.I.B.K3a to satisfy the requirement to select one knowledge element.

The References for each Task indicate the source material for Task elements. For example, in the Task element "Sources of weather data (e.g., National Weather Service, Flight Service) for flight planning purposes" (IR.I.B.K1), the applicant should be prepared for questions on any weather product presented in the references for that Task.

The FAA encourages applicants and instructors to use the ACS when preparing for the airman knowledge tests and practical tests. Evaluators must conduct the practical test in accordance with the current ACS and FAA regulations pursuant to 14 CFR part 61, section 61.43. If an applicant is entitled to credit for Areas of Operation previously passed as indicated on a Notice of Disapproval of Application or Letter of Discontinuance, evaluators shall use the ACS currently in effect on the date of the test.

The ground portion of the practical test allows the evaluator to determine whether the applicant is sufficiently prepared to advance to the flight portion of the practical test. The applicant must pass the ground portion of the practical test before beginning the flight portion. The oral questioning will continue throughout the entire practical test.

Combined Private/Instrument Test

Applicants for a combined Private Pilot Certificate with Instrument Rating, in accordance with 14 CFR part 61, section 61.65(a) and (g), must pass all areas designated in the Private Pilot for Airplane ACS and the Instrument Rating – Airplane ACS. Evaluators need not duplicate Tasks. For example, only one preflight demonstration would be required; however, the Preflight Task from the Instrument Rating – Airplane ACS would be more extensive than the Preflight Task from the Private Pilot for Airplane ACS to ensure readiness for Instrument Flight Rules (IFR) flight. Applicants for a combined test must present the applicable test reports.

A combined certificate and rating evaluation should be treated as one practical test, requiring only one application and resulting in only one temporary certificate, disapproval notice, or letter of discontinuance, as applicable. Failure of any Task will result in a failure of the entire test and application. Therefore, even if the deficient maneuver was instrument related and the performance of all visual flight rules (VFR) Tasks was determined to be satisfactory, the applicant will receive a notice of disapproval.

Instructor Responsibilities

The instructor trains and qualifies the applicant to meet the established standards for knowledge, risk management, and skill elements in all Tasks appropriate to the certificate and rating sought. The instructor should use this ACS and its references when preparing the applicant to take the practical test and when retraining the applicant to proficiency in any subject(s) missed on the knowledge test.

Evaluator Responsibilities

An evaluator includes the following:

- Aviation Safety Inspector (ASI);
- Pilot examiner (other than administrative pilot examiners);
- Training center evaluator (TCE);
- Chief instructor, assistant chief instructor, or check instructor of pilot school holding examining authority; or

- Instrument Flight Instructor (CFII) conducting an instrument proficiency check (IPC).

The evaluator who conducts the practical test verifies the applicant has met the aeronautical experience requirements specified for a certificate or rating before administering the test. During the practical test, the evaluator determines whether the applicant meets the established standards of aeronautical knowledge, risk management, and skills for the Tasks in the appropriate ACS.

The evaluator must develop a plan of action (POA) that includes all required Areas of Operation and Tasks and administer each practical test in English. The POA must include scenario(s) that evaluate as many of the required Areas of Operation and Tasks as possible. As a scenario unfolds during the test, the evaluator will introduce problems and simulate emergencies that test the applicant's ability. The evaluator has the discretion to modify the POA to accommodate unexpected situations as they arise or suspend and later resume a scenario to assess certain Tasks.

Prior to and throughout the evaluation, the evaluator ensures the applicant meets the FAA Aviation English Language Standard (AELS). An applicant must be able to communicate in English in a discernible and understandable manner with air traffic control (ATC), pilots, and others involved in preparing an aircraft for flight and operating an aircraft in flight. This communication may or may not involve radio communications. An applicant for an FAA certificate or rating issued in accordance with 14 CFR parts 61, 63, 65, or 107 who cannot hear or speak due to a medical deficiency may be eligible for an FAA certificate with specific operational limitations.

If the applicant's ability to meet the FAA AELS comes into question before starting the practical test, the evaluator will not begin the practical test. An evaluator other than an ASI will check the box, "Referred to FSO for Aviation English Language Standard Determination," located on the bottom of page 2 of the applicant's FAA Form 8710-1, Airman Certificate and/or Rating Application, or FAA Form 8710-11, Airman Certificate and/or Rating Application - Sport Pilot, as applicable. The evaluator will refer the applicant to the appropriate Flight Standards Office (FSO).

If the applicant's ability to meet the FAA AELS comes into question after the practical test begins, an evaluator who other than an ASI will discontinue the practical test and check the box, "Referred to FSO for Aviation English Language Standard Determination," on the application. The evaluator will also issue FAA Form 8060-5, Notice of Disapproval of Application, with the comment "Does Not Demonstrate FAA AELS" in addition to any unsatisfactory Task(s). The evaluator will refer the applicant to the appropriate FSO. ASIs conducting the practical test may assess an applicant's English language proficiency in accordance with FAA Order 8900.1.

In either case, the evaluator must complete and submit the application file through normal application procedures and evaluators other than an ASI notify the appropriate FSO of the referral.

If the ability of an FAA certificated airman comes into question prior to or during a required regulatory check (e.g., proficiency check) the evaluator other than an ASI will not continue the check or provide an endorsement indicating completion. The evaluator will refer the airman to the jurisdictional FAA field office for further determination of ability to meet the FAA AELS.

For additional information, reference AC 60-28, FAA English Language Standard for an FAA Certificate issued under 14 CFR parts 61, 63, 65, and 107, as amended.

The abbreviation(s) within parentheses immediately following a Task refers to the category and/or class airplane appropriate to that Task. The absence of a class indicates the Task is for all classes. The meaning of each abbreviation is as follows:

- ASEL—Airplane – Single-Engine Land
- ASES—Airplane – Single-Engine Sea
- AMEL—Airplane – Multiengine Land
- AMES—Airplane – Multiengine Sea

Possible Outcomes of the Test

A practical test has three possible outcomes: (1) Temporary Airman Certificate (satisfactory), (2) Notice of Disapproval of Application (unsatisfactory), or (3) Letter of Discontinuance.

If the evaluator determines that a Task is incomplete, or the outcome is uncertain, the evaluator must require the applicant to repeat that Task, or portions of that Task. This provision does not mean that instruction, practice, or the repetition of an unsatisfactory Task is permitted during the practical test.

Satisfactory Performance

Refer to 14 CFR part 61, section 61.43, for satisfactory performance requirements.

Satisfactory performance will result in the issuance of a temporary certificate.

Unsatisfactory Performance

If, in the judgment of the evaluator, the applicant does not meet the standards for any Task, the applicant fails the Task and associated Area of Operation and the evaluator issues a Notice of Disapproval of Application. The evaluator lists the Area(s) of Operation in which the applicant did not meet the standard, any Area(s) of Operation not tested, and the number of practical test failures. The evaluator should also list the Tasks failed or Tasks not tested within any unsatisfactory or partially completed Area(s) of Operation. 14 CFR part 61, section 61.43(c)–(f) provides additional unsatisfactory performance requirements and parameters.

Typical areas of unsatisfactory performance and grounds for disqualification include:

- Any action or lack of action by the applicant that requires corrective intervention by the evaluator to maintain safe flight.
- Failure to use proper and effective visual scanning techniques to clear the area before and while performing maneuvers.
- Consistently exceeding tolerances stated in the skill elements of the Task.
- Failure to take prompt corrective action when tolerances are exceeded.
- Failure to exercise risk management.

The evaluator or the applicant may end the test if the applicant fails a Task. The evaluator may continue the test only with the consent of the applicant. The applicant receives credit only for those Areas of Operation and the associated Tasks performed satisfactorily.

Letter of Discontinuance

Refer to 14 CFR part 61, section 61.43(e)(2) for conditions to issue a letter of discontinuance.

If discontinuing a practical test for reasons other than unsatisfactory performance (e.g., equipment failure, weather, illness), the evaluator must return all test paperwork to the applicant. The evaluator must prepare, sign, and issue a Letter of Discontinuance that lists those Areas of Operation the applicant successfully completed and the time period remaining to complete the test to receive credit for previously completed Areas of Operation. The evaluator should advise the applicant to present the Letter of Discontinuance to the evaluator when the practical test resumes in order to receive credit for the items successfully completed. The Letter of Discontinuance becomes part of the applicant's certification file.

Time Limit and Credit after a Discontinued Practical Test

Refer to 14 CFR part 61, sections 61.39(f) and 61.43(f) after issuance of a Letter of Discontinuance or Notice of Disapproval of Application.

Additional Rating Task Table

For an applicant who holds an instrument rating in another category and seeks an additional Instrument Airplane rating, the evaluator must evaluate that applicant in the Areas of Operation and Tasks listed in the Additional Rating Task Table. The evaluator may evaluate the applicant's competence in the remaining Areas of Operation and Tasks.

Addition of an Airplane Rating to an Existing Instrument Rating Certificate

The table below indicates the required Tasks for each Area of Operation tested in accordance with this ACS.

Required Area of Operation	Required Task(s)
I	None
II	A,C
III	None
IV	All
V	None
VI	All
VII	All
VIII	All

Note: *In Area of Operation VII, Emergency Operations, Tasks B and C apply to multiengine tests only.*

The removal of the "Airplane Multiengine VFR Only" limitation, at the private pilot or commercial pilot certificate level, requires an applicant to satisfactorily perform the following Area of Operation and Tasks from the Instrument Rating – Airplane ACS: Area of Operation VII, Emergency Operations, in a multiengine airplane that has a manufacturer's published VMC speed.

- Task B: One Engine Inoperative during Straight-and-Level Flight and Turns (AMEL, AMES)
- Task C: Instrument Approach and Landing with an Inoperative Engine (Simulated) (AMEL, AMES)

Instrument Proficiency Check

14 CFR part 61, section 61.57(d) sets forth the requirements for an instrument proficiency check (IPC). Evaluators conducting an IPC must ensure the pilot meets the standards established in this ACS. As a minimum, the applicant must demonstrate the ability to perform the Tasks listed in the table below. The person giving the check should develop a scenario that incorporates as many required Tasks as practical to assess the pilot's aeronautical decision making (ADM) and risk management skills.

Required Area of Operation	Required Task(s)
I	None
II	None
III	B
IV	B
V	A
VI	All
VII	B,C,D
VIII	All

Note: *In Area of Operation VII, Emergency Operations, Tasks B and C apply to multiengine tests only.*

An Advanced Aviation Training Device (AATD) can be utilized for the majority of the IPC as specified in the Letter of Authorization issued for the device. However, the circling approach, the landing Task, and the multiengine airplane Tasks must be accomplished in an aircraft or FFS (Level B, C, or D). A Basic Aviation Training Device (BATD) cannot be used for any part of the IPC.

Refer to Advisory Circular (AC) 61-98 (as amended), Currency Requirements and Guidance for the Flight Review and Instrument Proficiency Check, as amended for information on conducting an IPC. The AC can be found at: www.faa.gov.

Appendix 2: Safety of Flight

General

Safety of flight must be the prime consideration at all times. The evaluator, applicant, and crew must be continually alert for other traffic. If performing aspects of a given maneuver, such as emergency procedures, would jeopardize safety, the evaluator will ask the applicant to simulate that portion of the maneuver. The evaluator will assess the applicant's use of visual scanning and collision avoidance procedures throughout the entire test.

Stall and Spin Awareness

During flight training and testing, the applicant and the instructor or evaluator must always recognize and avoid operations that could lead to an inadvertent stall or spin and inadvertent loss of control.

Use of Checklists

Throughout the practical test, the applicant is evaluated on the use of an appropriate checklist.

Assessing proper checklist use depends upon the specific Task. In all cases, the evaluator should determine whether the applicant demonstrates CRM, appropriately divides attention, and uses proper visual scanning. In some situations, reading the actual checklist may be impractical or unsafe. In such cases, the evaluator should assess the applicant's performance of published or recommended immediate action "memory" items along with their review of the appropriate checklist once conditions permit.

In a single-pilot airplane, the applicant should demonstrate the crew resource management (CRM) principles described as single-pilot resource management (SRM). Proper use depends on the specific Task being evaluated. If the use of the checklist while accomplishing elements of an Objective would be either unsafe or impractical in a single-pilot operation, the applicant should review the checklist after accomplishing the elements.

Positive Exchange of Flight Controls

A clear understanding of who has control of the aircraft must exist. Prior to flight, the pilots involved should conduct a briefing that includes reviewing the procedures for exchanging flight controls.

The FAA recommends a positive three-step process for exchanging flight controls between pilots:

- When one pilot seeks to have the other pilot take control of the aircraft, they will say, "You have the flight controls."
- The second pilot acknowledges immediately by saying, "I have the flight controls."
- The first pilot again says, "You have the flight controls," and visually confirms the exchange.

Pilots should follow this procedure during any exchange of flight controls, including any occurrence during the practical test. The FAA also recommends that both pilots use a visual check to verify that the exchange has occurred. Doubt as to who is flying the aircraft should not occur.

Use of Distractions

Numerous studies indicate that many accidents have occurred when the pilot has been distracted during critical phases of flight. The evaluator should incorporate realistic distractions during the flight portion of the practical test to evaluate the pilot's situational awareness and ability to utilize proper control technique while dividing attention both inside and outside the flight deck.

Aeronautical Decision-Making, Risk Management, Crew Resource Management, and Single-Pilot Resource Management

Throughout the practical test, the evaluator must assess the applicant's ability to use sound aeronautical decision-making procedures in order to identify hazards and mitigate risk. The evaluator must accomplish this requirement by reference to the risk management elements of the given Task(s), and by developing scenarios that incorporate and combine Tasks appropriate to assessing the applicant's risk management in making safe aeronautical decisions. For example, the evaluator may develop a scenario that incorporates weather decisions and performance planning.

In assessing the applicant's performance, the evaluator should take note of the applicant's use of CRM and, if appropriate, SRM. CRM/SRM is the set of competencies that includes situational awareness, communication skills, teamwork, task allocation, and decision-making within a comprehensive framework of standard operating procedures (SOP). SRM specifically refers to the management of all resources onboard the aircraft, as well as outside resources available to the single pilot.

Multiengine Considerations

For instrument practical tests conducted in multiengine aircraft, the evaluator must discuss with the applicant the methods for simulating an engine failure in accordance with the aircraft manufacturer's recommended procedures during the required preflight briefing.

Appendix 3: Aircraft, Equipment, and Operational Requirements & Limitations

Aircraft Requirements & Limitations

If the aircraft has inoperative equipment and can be operated in accordance with 14 CFR part 91, section 91.213, it must be determined if any inoperative instruments or equipment are required to complete the practical test. The inoperative equipment must not interfere with practical test requirements. Applicants testing in a multiengine airplane must provide a multiengine airplane with a published VMC unless the airman's certificate has a center thrust limitation.

Equipment Requirements & Limitations

The aircraft must meet the requirements as outlined in 14 CFR part 61, section 61.45.

To assist in management of the aircraft during the practical test, the applicant is expected to demonstrate automation management skills by utilizing installed, available, or airborne equipment such as autopilot, avionics and systems displays, and/or a flight management system (FMS). The evaluator is expected to test the applicant's knowledge of the systems that are available or installed and operative during both the ground and flight portions of the practical test. If the applicant has trained using a portable electronic flight bag (EFB) to display charts and data and wishes to use the EFB during the practical test, the applicant is expected to demonstrate appropriate knowledge, risk management, and skill appropriate to its use.

If the practical test involves maneuvering the aircraft solely by reference to instruments, the applicant is required by 14 CFR part 61, section 61.45(d)(2) to provide an appropriate view limiting device acceptable to the Administrator. The applicant and the evaluator should establish a procedure as to when and how this device should be donned and removed and brief this procedure before the flight. This device must prevent the applicant from having visual reference outside the aircraft, but it must not restrict the evaluator's ability to see and avoid other traffic. The use of the device does not apply to specific elements within a Task when there is a requirement for visual references.

Use of Flight Simulation Training Devices (FSTD)

Applicants for a pilot certificate or rating can accomplish all or part of a practical test or proficiency check in an FSTD qualified under 14 CFR part 60, which includes full flight simulators (FFS) or flight training devices (FTD), only when conducted within an FAA-approved training program. Each operational rule part identifies additional requirements for the approval and use of FSTDs in an FAA-approved training program.

Credit for Pilot Time in an FSTD

14 CFR part 61 and part 141 specify the minimum experience requirements for each certificate or rating sought. 14 CFR part 61 and the appendices to part 141 specify the maximum amount of FFS or FTD flight training time an applicant can apply toward those experience requirements.

Use of Aviation Training Devices (ATD)

Applicants for a pilot certificate or rating cannot use an ATD to accomplish a practical test, a 14 CFR part 61, section 61.58 proficiency check, or the flight portion of a 14 CFR part 61, section 61.57 flight review. An ATD is defined in 14 CFR part 61, section 61.1.

The FAA's General Aviation and Commercial Division evaluates and approves ATDs as permitted under 14 CFR part 61, section 61.4(c) and FAA Order 8900.1. Each ATD is then issued an FAA letter of authorization (LOA) that is valid for 60 calendar months. The LOA for each ATD lists the pilot time credit allowances and associated limitations.

The Pilot Training and Certification Group public website provides a list of the FAA-approved ATDs and the associated manufacturer.

Credit for Pilot Time in an ATD

14 CFR part 61 and part 141 specify the minimum experience requirements for each certificate or rating sought. 14 CFR part 61 and the appendices to part 141 specify the maximum amount of ATD flight training time an applicant can apply toward those experience requirements. The LOA for each FAA-approved ATD lists the pilot time credit allowances and the associated limitations.

Evaluators must request an applicant to provide a copy of the manufacturer's LOA when using ATD flight training time credit to meet the minimum experience requirements for an airman pilot certificate, rating, or privilege.

Operational Requirements, Limitations, & Task Information

V. Navigation Systems

Task A. Intercepting and Tracking Navigational Systems and DME Arcs

The evaluator may not select DME arcs, unless charted and available (including use of RNAV substitution techniques, if appropriate).

VI. Instrument Approach Procedures

Use of Area Navigation (RNAV) or Required Navigation Performance (RNP) Navigation System

For practical tests conducted in an aircraft equipped with an installed, instrument flight rules (IFR)-approved RNAV or required navigational performance (RNP) system, or in a flight simulation training device (FSTD) equipped to replicate an installed, IFR-approved RNAV or RNP system, the applicant must demonstrate approach proficiency using that system. The applicant may use a suitable RNAV system on conventional procedures and routes as described in the Aeronautical Information Manual (AIM) to accomplish ACS tasks on conventional approach procedures, as appropriate.

Vertical or Lateral Deviation Standard

The standard is to allow no more than a ¾ scale deflection of either the vertical or lateral deviation indications during the final approach. As markings on flight instruments vary, a ¾ scale deflection of either vertical or lateral guidance is deemed to occur when it is displaced ¾ of the distance that it may be deflected from the indication representing that the aircraft is on the correct flight path.

Task A. Non-precision Approach

A non-precision approach is a standard instrument approach procedure to a published minimum descent altitude without approved vertical guidance. The applicant may use navigation systems that display advisory vertical guidance during non-precision approach operations, if available.

The evaluator must select and the applicant must accomplish at least two different non-precision approaches in simulated or actual instrument meteorological conditions:

- At least one procedure must include a course reversal maneuver (e.g., procedure turn, holding in lieu, or the course reversal from an initial approach fix on a Terminal Area Arrival).

- The applicant must accomplish at least one procedure from an initial approach fix without the use of autopilot and without the assistance of radar vectors. During this Task, flying without using the autopilot does not prevent use of the yaw damper and flight director.

- The applicant must fly one procedure with reference to backup or partial panel instrumentation or navigation display, depending on the aircraft's instrument avionics configuration, representing a realistic failure mode(s) for the equipment used.

The evaluator has discretion to have the applicant perform a landing or a missed approach at the completion of each approach.

Task B. Precision Approach

The applicant must accomplish a precision approach to the decision altitude (DA) using aircraft navigational equipment for centerline and vertical guidance in simulated or actual instrument meteorological conditions. A precision approach is a standard instrument approach procedure to a published decision altitude using provided approved vertical guidance.

The evaluator has discretion to have the applicant perform a landing or a missed approach at the completion of each approach.

U.S. Department
of Transportation

**Federal Aviation
Administration**

Airman Certification Standards
Companion Guide for Pilots

November 2023

Flight Standards Service
Washington, DC 20591

Foreword

The Federal Aviation Administration (FAA) developed this Airman Certification Standards Companion Guide FAA-G-ACS-2, for use with the Airman Certification Standards (ACS) for pilot certification. This guide, along with the regulatory material in the ACS, may assist an applicant preparing for the knowledge and practical test(s) that lead to pilot certification. This document is intended only to provide clarity to the public regarding existing requirements under the law or agency policies. The contents of this document do not have the force and effect of law and are not meant to bind the public in any way.

This guide and the ACS are available for download from www.faa.gov.

Comments regarding this document may be emailed to acsptsinquiries@faa.gov.

Revision History

Document #	Description	Date
FAA-G-ACS-2	Airman Certification Standards Companion Guide for Pilots	November 2023

Table of Contents

Why the FAA Created this Guide

The Federal Aviation Administration (FAA) publishes the Airman Certification Standards (ACS) to communicate the aeronautical knowledge, risk management, and flight proficiency standards for various certificates and ratings available to airmen. The ACSs are incorporated by reference into 14 CFR part 61; therefore, the material contained in the ACS is regulatory. This guide, FAA-G-ACS-2, provides additional information to the regulated community to facilitate airman testing. The ACS complies with the safety management system (SMS) framework that the FAA uses to mitigate risks associated with airman certification training and testing. Specifically, the ACS, incorporated by reference (IBR) into the Federal Aviation Regulations, conforms to four functional components of an SMS:

- Safety Policy—Each ACS specifies the Tasks selected by the FAA from the regulatory Areas of Operation. Evaluators formulate a Plan of Action that determines if an applicant can operate safely within the NAS. The ACS represents the FAA's commitment to continually improve safety by including risk management elements in addition to knowledge and skill elements;

- Safety Risk Management that complies with the Administrative Procedures Act (APA) allows the FAA to work with internal and external stakeholders during document formulation. The public at large and stakeholders have an additional chance to provide input during public comment periods;

- Safety Assurance processes ensure a methodical and reasoned incorporation of changes arising from safety recommendations or new developments in aviation; and

- Safety Promotion in the form of engagement and discussion between both external stakeholders (e.g., the aviation training industry) and the FAA policy divisions going forward will determine the content of any ACS that publishes in a Notice of Proposed Rulemaking.

The FAA develops the ACS documents along with associated guidance and updated reference material in collaboration with a diverse group of aviation training experts. The goal is to drive a systematic approach to all components of the airman certification system, including knowledge test question development and conduct of the practical test. The FAA acknowledges and appreciates the many hours that these aviation experts have contributed toward this goal. This level of collaboration, a hallmark of a robust safety culture, strengthens and enhances aviation safety at every level of the airman certification system.

Note: This document does not apply to the Practical Test Standards.

The Non-Regulatory Material in this Guide

This guide provides test preparatory information for an applicant seeking a certificate or rating. This guide also provides a list of references and abbreviations/acronyms used in any ACS and a practical test checklist for use by an applicant. The material in this guide is non-regulatory and may contain terms such as should or may:

- Should indicates actions that are recommended, but not regulatory.
- May is used in a permissive sense to state authority or permission to do the act prescribed.

This document is not legally binding and will not be relied upon by the FAA as a basis for affirmative enforcement action or other administrative penalty. Conformity with the guidance is voluntary only and nonconformity will not affect rights and obligations under existing statutes and regulations.

Section 1: Knowledge Test Eligibility, Description, and Registration

Eligibility

For detailed airman knowledge test eligibility and applicable prerequisites, applicants should refer to the 14 CFR part 61 rules that apply to a specific certificate or rating.

Steps for Knowledge Test Registration

Step 1. Obtain an FAA Tracking Number

The FAA Airman Knowledge Test registration system requires the applicant to have an FAA Tracking Number (FTN). Applicants may obtain an FTN through the Integrated Airman Certification and Rating Application (IACRA) website.

This video describes creating an IACRA account and obtaining an FTN. The specific instructions begin at the 14-minute mark.

Step 2. Create an Account with PSI

After obtaining an FTN, applicants should create an account with the FAA's contracted testing vendor, PSI, a professional testing company which operates hundreds of test centers. Visit PSI's website for information on authorized airman knowledge test centers and how to register, schedule, and pay for an Airman Knowledge Test:

> **Note:** *The IACRA and PSI systems share data that verifies the applicant's FTN and name based on the information input into IACRA by the applicant. The PSI system does not allow applicants to make changes to their name. Applicants who need to make a correction to their name should process that correction in the IACRA system. The applicant's name correction will appear in the PSI system once the applicant logs back into the PSI system and refreshes their account.*

Step 3. Select Test and Testing Center

After obtaining an FTN and creating an account with PSI, applicants may schedule knowledge tests. The PSI system walks the applicant through the process to select a test center in their area and select one or more specific knowledge tests.

Step 4. Select an Available Time Slot

After selecting the test center and test, the applicant may select a date and time slot.

Step 5. Pay for Test

After selecting an available time slot, the PSI system prompts the applicant to pay for the test. After completing this step, the applicant receives an automated email confirmation from PSI.

Applicants are required to meet any applicable Airman Knowledge Test eligibility requirements before arriving at a test center to take a specific knowledge test.

Testing Procedures for Applicants Requesting Special Accommodations

Applicants may request a special accommodation for their airman knowledge test through the PSI test registration and scheduling process. The process allows the applicant to select the specific accommodation(s) needed in accordance with the Americans with Disabilities Act (ADA). The PSI special accommodations team will work with the applicant and the selected testing center to provide appropriate accommodation(s). The PSI special accommodations team may request medical documentation for verification.

Acceptable Forms of Identification

14 CFR part 61, section 61.35, requires an applicant for a knowledge test to have proper identification at the time of application. Before beginning an Airman Knowledge Test, test center personnel will ask to see the applicant's state or federal government-issued photo identification. The identification must contain the applicant's photograph, signature, and date of birth. If the applicant's permanent mailing address is a PO Box number, the applicant must provide a current residential address.

Acceptable Forms of Applicant Address Verification

The table below provides examples of acceptable identification.

All Applicants	U.S. Citizens & Resident Aliens	Non-U.S. Citizens
Identification information must be: ✓ valid ✓ current Identification must include **all** of the following information: ✓ photo ✓ date of birth ✓ signature ✓ physical, residential address	✓ Identification card issued by any **U.S.** state, territory, or government entity (e.g., driver permit or license, government identification card, or military identification card) **or** ✓ Passport **or** ✓ Alien residency card	✓ Passport **and** ✓ Driver permit or license issued by a U.S. state or territory **or** ✓ Identification card issued by any government entity

Airman Knowledge Test Description

The airman knowledge test consists of multiple-choice questions. A single correct response exists for each test question. A correct response to one question does not depend upon, or influence, the correct response to another.

Taking the Knowledge Test

Before starting the actual test, the test center provides an applicant with the opportunity to practice navigating the test software. This practice or tutorial session may include sample questions to familiarize the applicant with the look and feel of the software (e.g., selecting an answer, marking a question for later review, monitoring time remaining for the test, and other features of the testing software). PSI also provides sample tests for registered users on their website.

Acceptable and Unacceptable Materials

The applicant may use the following aids, reference materials, and test materials when taking the knowledge test provided the material does not include actual test questions or answers:

Acceptable Materials	Unacceptable Materials	Notes
Supplement book provided by the proctor	Written materials that are handwritten, printed, or electronic	Testing centers may provide calculators and/or deny the use of personal calculators.
All models of aviation-oriented calculators or small electronic calculators that perform only arithmetic functions	Electronic calculators incorporating permanent or continuous type memory circuits without erasure capability	Proctor may prohibit the use of an applicant's calculator if the proctor is unable to determine the calculator's erasure capability
Calculators with simple programmable memories, which allow the addition to, subtraction from, or retrieval of one number from the memory, or simple functions, such as square root and percentages	Magnetic Cards, magnetic tapes, modules, computer chips, or any other device upon which pre-written programs or information related to the test can be stored and retrieved	Printouts of data should be surrendered at the completion of the test if the calculator incorporates this design feature
Scales, straightedges, protractors, plotters, navigation computers, blank log sheets, holding pattern entry aids, and electronic or mechanical calculators that are directly related to the test	Dictionaries	Before, and upon completion of the test, while in the presence of the proctor, actuate the ON/OFF switch or RESET button, and perform any other function that ensures erasure of any data stored in memory circuits
Manufacturer's permanently inscribed instructions on the front and back of such aids (e.g., formulas, conversions, regulations, signals, weather data, holding pattern diagrams, frequencies, weight and balance formulas, and air traffic control procedures)	Any booklet or manual containing instructions related to the use of test aids	Proctor makes the final determination regarding aids, reference materials, and test materials

Test Taking Tips

When taking a knowledge test, applicants should:

- Read the test instructions carefully;
- Mark difficult questions for later review in order to use the available time efficiently;
- Examine graphs and notes that pertain to the question;
- Request and mark a printed copy of any graph while computing answers, if needed;
- Understand that since only one answer is complete and correct, the other possible answers are either incomplete or erroneous;
- Answer each question in accordance with the current regulations and guidance publications; and
- Answer all the questions before time allotted for the test expires.
- Review 14 CFR part 61, section 61.37 regarding cheating or other unauthorized conduct.

Section 2: Airman Knowledge Test Report

Upon completion of the knowledge test, the test center issues a printed Airman Knowledge Test Report (AKTR) to the applicant, which documents the applicant's test score and lists a code for any questions answered incorrectly. The applicant should retain the original AKTR. During the oral portion of a practical test, the evaluator reviews the AKTR, and assesses any noted areas of deficiency.

Applicant Name Considerations for the Airman Knowledge Test Report and the Practical Test

The FAA compares the applicant's name on the AKTR with the name on the practical test application form when examining certificate and rating applications and before issuing a permanent certificate to the applicant. If an incorrect middle initial, spelling variant, or different middle name is on the AKTR or if there is a first name variation of any kind between the AKTR and the formal application for a certificate or rating, the evaluator for the practical test should attach an explanation and a copy of the applicant's photo identification to the IACRA or paper application. An IACRA application cannot be processed if the applicant's last name or suffix (e.g., Jr., Sr.) on the AKTR does not match the name recorded on the application form. In this case, the applicant should use a paper application, and the evaluator should include an explanation and copy of the applicant's photo identification to avoid a correction notice.

Retesting After Failure of AKTR

An applicant retesting after the failure of any Airman Knowledge Test may retest with appropriate authorization. The applicant should bring the applicable AKTR indicating failure to the test center, along with an endorsement from an Authorized Instructor who gave the applicant the required additional training in accordance with 14 CFR part 61, section 61.49. The endorsement certifies that the applicant is competent to pass the knowledge test.

Knowledge Test Codes During Transition from PTS To ACS

When a PTS is the effective standard for a specific certificate or rating, the applicant receives an Airman Knowledge Test Report with pilot (PLT) codes that correspond to any knowledge test question(s) the applicant answered incorrectly. For example: PLT044.

For knowledge tests taken after an ACS becomes the effective standard for a specific certificate or rating, the test center issues an AKTR with ACS codes that correspond to any knowledge test question(s) the applicant answered incorrectly. For example: CA.I.A.K1

During a period of transition after an ACS replaces a PTS, an applicant could possess a valid AKTR with PLT codes. When this occurs, instructors and evaluators can continue to use PLT codes in conjunction with the appropriate ACS for targeting training and retesting of missed knowledge subject areas by looking up the PLT code(s) in the Learning Statement Reference Guide.

After noting the subject area(s) for the PLT codes, instructors and evaluators should check or test the applicant's understanding of that material in the context of the appropriate ACS Area(s) of Operation and Task(s).

> **Note:** Test codes for the Fundamentals of Instructing knowledge test are the same for all instructor certificates and will issue with ACS codes after the first instructor ACS becomes effective.

ACS Archived Test Codes

As a result of updates made to an ACS, an AKTR may contain one or more archived ACS codes. These codes are indicated as archived within the ACS. For example:

       PA.VIII.E.K1a   Archived.

Use of archived codes in the ACS avoids code shifting that could create ambiguity when looking up ACS codes listed on an AKTR. An unexpired AKTR may span ACS revisions and ACS codes may archive after an applicant takes a knowledge test. Therefore, an applicant, instructor, or evaluator may need to interpret one or more archived ACS codes on an AKTR. Individuals can refer to the ACS revision in effect on the date of the knowledge test or to section 8 of this guide for archived ACS codes and the associated element text.

Use of archived codes in the ACS avoids code shifting that could create ambiguity when looking up ACS codes listed on an AKTR. An unexpired AKTR may span ACS revisions and ACS codes may archive after an applicant takes a knowledge test. Therefore, an applicant, instructor, or evaluator may need to interpret one or more archived ACS codes on an AKTR. Individuals can refer to the ACS revision in effect on the date of the knowledge test or to Section 8 of this guide for archived ACS codes and the associated element text. For example, the archived ACS code for Private Pilot Airplane element PA.VIII.E.K1a is noted in Section 8 of this guide as: Sensitivity, limitations, and potential errors in unusual attitudes.

Obtaining a Duplicate AKTR

If the applicant's knowledge test was taken on or after January 13, 2020, the applicant can print a duplicate or expired test report (AKTR) by visiting the PSI website.

If the knowledge test was taken on or before January 10, 2020, the applicant should follow 14 CFR, section 61.29 for replacement of a lost or destroyed AKTR.

Section 3: ACS Risk Management

Risk management involves perception of hazards, the ability to process the probability and severity of outcomes associated with any hazard, and performance of appropriate risk mitigation as needed to preserve the desired margin of safety.

Previous editions of the ACS often used elements for evaluation of risk management as encompassing a failure to do something. Many of these "failure to act" elements mimicked skill elements and limited an evaluator's opportunity to thoroughly examine an applicant's understanding of risk management.

For example, see elements R1 and S2 from the Private Pilot — Airplane Airman Certification Standards (FAA-S-ACS-6B with Change 1) in the excerpt below:

Task	C. Systems and Equipment Malfunctions
References	FAA-H-8083-2, FAA-H-8083-3; POH/AFM
Objective	To determine that the applicant exhibits satisfactory knowledge, risk management, and skills associated with system and equipment malfunctions appropriate to the airplane provided for the practical test and analyzing the situation and take appropriate action for simulated emergencies.
Knowledge	The applicant demonstrates understanding of:
PA.IX.C.K1	Partial or complete power loss related to the specific powerplant, including:
PA.IX.C.K1a	a. Engine roughness or overheat
PA.IX.C.K1b	b. Carburetor or induction icing
PA.IX.C.K1c	c. Loss of oil pressure
PA.IX.C.K1d	d. Fuel starvation
PA.IX.C.K2	System and equipment malfunctions specific to the airplane, including:
PA.IX.C.K2a	a. Electrical malfunction
PA.IX.C.K2b	b. Vacuum/pressure and associated flight instrument malfunctions
PA.IX.C.K2c	c. Pitot/static system malfunction
PA.IX.C.K2d	d. Electronic flight deck display malfunction
PA.IX.C.K2e	e. Landing gear or flap malfunction
PA.IX.C.K2f	f. Inoperative trim
PA.IX.C.K3	Smoke/fire/engine compartment fire.
PA.IX.C.K4	Any other system specific to the airplane (e.g., supplemental oxygen, deicing).
PA.IX.C.K5	Inadvertent door or window opening.
Risk Management	The applicant demonstrates the ability to identify, assess and mitigate risks, encompassing:
PA.IX.C.R1	Failure to use the proper checklist for a system or equipment malfunction.
PA.IX.C.R2	Distractions, loss of situational awareness, or improper task management.
Skills	The applicant demonstrates the ability to:
PA.IX.C.S1	Describe appropriate action for simulated emergencies specified by the evaluator, from at least three of the elements or sub-elements listed in K1 through K5 above.
PA.IX.C.S2	Complete the appropriate checklist.

The FAA reworded risk elements that describe a Failure to... (or similar phrases) with language permitting an open-ended examination of risk management by the evaluator. See element R2 in the excerpt below (image for illustration purposes only):

Task C. Systems and Equipment Malfunctions

References: FAA-H-8083-2, FAA-H-8083-3, FAA-H-8083-25; POH/AFM

Objective: To determine the applicant exhibits satisfactory knowledge, risk management, and skills associated with system and equipment malfunctions appropriate to the airplane provided for the practical test.

Knowledge:	The applicant demonstrates understanding of:
PA.IX.C.K1	Causes of partial or complete power loss related to the specific type of powerplant(s).
PA.IX.C.K1a	a. [Archived]
PA.IX.C.K1b	b. [Archived]
PA.IX.C.K1c	c. [Archived]
PA.IX.C.K1d	d. [Archived]
PA.IX.C.K2	System and equipment malfunctions specific to the aircraft, including:
PA.IX.C.K2a	a. Electrical malfunction
PA.IX.C.K2b	b. Vacuum/pressure and associated flight instrument malfunctions
PA.IX.C.K2c	c. Pitot-static system malfunction
PA.IX.C.K2d	d. Electronic flight deck display malfunction
PA.IX.C.K2e	e. Landing gear or flap malfunction
PA.IX.C.K2f	f. Inoperative trim
PA.IX.C.K3	Causes and remedies for smoke or fire onboard the aircraft.
PA.IX.C.K4	Any other system specific to the aircraft (e.g., supplemental oxygen, deicing).
PA.IX.C.K5	Inadvertent door or window opening.
Risk Management:	The applicant is able to identify, assess, and mitigate risk associated with:
PA.IX.C.R1	Checklist usage for a system or equipment malfunction.
PA.IX.C.R2	Distractions, task prioritization, loss of situational awareness, or disorientation.
PA.IX.C.R3	Undesired aircraft state.
PA.IX.C.R4	Startle response.
Skills:	The applicant exhibits the skill to:
PA.IX.C.S1	Determine appropriate action for simulated emergencies specified by the evaluator, from at least three of the elements or sub-elements listed in K1 through K5.
PA.IX.C.S2	Complete the appropriate checklist(s).

Section 4: Flight Instructor Applicant Considerations

Flight Instructor ACS Information

Flight Instructor ACS documents include sections that define the acceptable standards for knowledge, risk management, and skills unique to an instructor certificate or rating.

Knowledge elements often begin with "The applicant demonstrates instructional knowledge by describing and explaining..." Instructional knowledge means the instructor applicant can effectively present the what, how, and why involved with the task elements using techniques described in the fundamentals of instructing (FOI) area of operation in an instructor ACS.

The Fundamentals of Instructing (FOI), Area of Operation I, Task F: Elements of Effective Teaching that include Risk Management and Accident Prevention focuses on teaching risk management and on those risks encountered by a flight instructor while providing in-flight instruction.

Instructor applicants deal with additional risk management on several levels. These include teaching risk management in the classroom and mitigation of risk during flight instruction.

Note that the FOI sections in each instructor ACS are identical and use the same element codes. This makes it possible to use the same FOI elements for every instructor ACS.

Section 5: References

The ACS are based on the following 14 CFR parts, FAA guidance documents, manufacturer's publications, and other documents.

Note: *Users should reference the current edition of the reference documents listed below. The current edition of all FAA publications can be found at www.faa.gov.*

Reference	Title
14 CFR part 1	Definitions and Abbreviations
14 CFR part 23	Airworthiness Standards: Normal Category Airplanes
14 CFR part 25	Airworthiness Standards: Transport Category Airplanes
14 CFR part 27	Airworthiness Standards: Normal Category Rotorcraft
14 CFR part 29	Airworthiness Standards: Transport Category Rotorcraft
14 CFR part 39	Airworthiness Directives
14 CFR part 43	Maintenance, Preventive Maintenance, Rebuilding, and Alteration
14 CFR part 61	Certification: Pilots, Flight Instructors, and Ground Instructors
14 CFR part 63	Certification: Flight Crewmembers other than Pilots
14 CFR part 65	Certification: Airmen Other Than Flightcrew Members
14 CFR part 67	Medical Standards and Certification
14 CFR part 68	Requirements for Operating Certain Small Aircraft Without a Medical Certificate
14 CFR part 71	Designation of Class A, B, C, D, and E Airspace Areas; Air Traffic Service Routes; and Reporting Points
14 CFR part 91	General Operating and Flight Rules
14 CFR part 93	Special Air Traffic Rules
14 CFR part 97	Standard Instrument Procedures
14 CFR part 117	Flight and Duty Limitations and Rest Requirements: Flightcrew Members
14 CFR part 119	Certification: Air Carriers and Commercial Operators
14 CFR part 121	Operating Requirements: Domestic, Flag, and Supplemental Operations
14 CFR part 135	Operating Requirements: Commuter and on Demand Operations and Rules Governing Persons on Board Such Aircraft
49 CFR part 830	Notification and Reporting of Aircraft Accidents or Incidents and Overdue Aircraft, and Preservation of Aircraft Wreckage, Mail, Cargo, and Records
AC 00-30	Clear Air Turbulence Avoidance
AC 00-46	Aviation Safety Reporting Program
AC 20-117	Hazards Following Ground Deicing and Ground Operations in Conditions Conducive to Aircraft Icing
AC 29-2	Certification of Transport Category Rotorcraft
AC 60-22	Aeronautical Decision Making
AC 60-28	FAA English Language Standard for an FAA Certificate Issued Under 14 CFR Parts 61, 63, 65, and 107
AC 61-65	Certification: Pilots and Flight and Ground Instructors

Reference	Title
AC 61-67	Stall and Spin Awareness Training
AC 61-107	Aircraft Operations at Altitudes Above 25,000 Feet Mean Sea Level or Mach Numbers Greater Than .75
AC 61-138	Airline Transport Pilot Certification Training Program
AC 61-140	Autorotation Training
AC 68-1	BasicMed
AC 90-48	Pilots' Role in Collision Avoidance
AC 90-95	Unanticipated Right Yaw in Helicopters
AC 90-100	U.S Terminal and En Route Area Navigation (RNAV) Operations
AC 90-105	Approval Guidance for RNP Operations and Barometric Vertical Navigation in the U.S. National Airspace System and in Oceanic and Remote Continental Airspace
AC 90-107	Guidance for Localizer Performance with Vertical Guidance and Localizer Performance without Vertical Guidance Approach Operations in the U.S. National Airspace System
AC 90-117	Data Link Communications
AC 91.21-1	Use of Portable Electronic Devices Aboard Aircraft
AC 91-32	Safety in and Around Helicopters
AC 91-55	Reduction of Electrical System Failures Following Aircraft Engine Starting
AC 91-73	Parts 91 and 135 Single Pilot, Flight School Procedures During Taxi Operations
AC 91-74	Pilot Guide: Flight in Icing Conditions
AC 91-78	Use of Class 1 or Class 2 Electronic Flight Bag (EFB)
AC 91-79	Mitigating the Risks of a Runway Overrun Upon Landing
AC 91-92	Pilot's Guide to a Preflight Briefing
AC 120-27	Aircraft Weight and Balance Control
AC 120-51	Crew Resource Management Training
AC 120-57	Surface Movement Guidance and Control System
AC 120-58	Pilot Guide Large Aircraft Ground Deicing
AC 120-60	Ground Deicing and Anti-icing Program
AC 120-66	Aviation Safety Action Program (ASAP)
AC 120-71	Standard Operating Procedures and Pilot Monitoring Duties for Flight Deck Crewmembers
AC 120-74	Parts 91, 121, 125, and 135 Flightcrew Procedures During Taxi Operations
AC 120-76	Authorization for Use of Electronic Flight Bags
AC 120-82	Flight Operational Quality Assurance (FOQA)
AC 120-90	Line Operations Safety Audit (LOSA)
AC 120-100	Basics of Aviation Fatigue
AC 120-101	Part 121 Air Carrier Operational Control
AC 120-108	Continuous Descent Final Approach

Reference	Title
AC 120-109	Stall Prevention and Recovery Training
AC 120-111	Upset Prevention and Recovery Training
AC 135-17	Pilot Guide - Small Aircraft Ground Deicing
AFM	Airplane Flight Manual
AIM	Aeronautical Information Manual
AC 120-100	Basics of Aviation Fatigue
AC 120-101	Part 121 Air Carrier Operational Control
AC 120-108	Continuous Descent Final Approach
AC 120-109	Stall Prevention and Recovery Training
AC 120-111	Upset Prevention and Recovery Training
AC 135-17	Pilot Guide - Small Aircraft Ground Deicing
AFM	Airplane Flight Manual
AIM	Aeronautical Information Manual
Applicable Manufacturer's Equipment Supplement(s)	Manufacturer's Equipment Supplement(s)
Appropriate Manufacturer's Safety Notices	Safety Notices
Chart Supplements	Chart Supplements
Digital-Visual Charts (d-VC)	Digital-Visual Charts (d-VC)
FAA-H-8083-1	Aircraft Weight and Balance Handbook
FAA-H-8083-2	Risk Management Handbook
FAA-H-8083-3	Airplane Flying Handbook
FAA-H-8083-9	Aviation Instructor's Handbook
FAA-H-8083-15	Instrument Flying Handbook
FAA-H-8083-16	Instrument Procedures Handbook
FAA-H-8083-21	Helicopter Flying Handbook
FAA-H-8083-23	Seaplane, Skiplane, and Float/Ski Equipped Helicopter Operations Handbook
FAA-H-8083-25	Pilot's Handbook of Aeronautical Knowledge
FAA-H-8083-28	Aviation Weather Handbook
FAA Order 8130.2	Airworthiness Certification of Aircraft
FAA-P-8740-66	Flying Light Twins Safely
FSB Report (type specific)	Flight Standardization Board Report (if available)
Helicopter Route Charts	Helicopter Route Charts
IFR Enroute Charts	IFR Enroute Low Altitude and IFR Enroute High Altitude Charts
NOTAMs	Notices to Air Missions
PDC	Profile Descent Charts

Reference	Title
POH/AFM	Pilot's Operating Handbook/FAA-Approved Airplane Flight Manual
POH/Flight Manual	Pilot's Operating Handbook/FAA-Approved Flight Manual
POH/RFM	Pilot's Operating Handbook/FAA-Approved Rotorcraft Flight Manual
QRH	Quick Reference Handbook
SAFO 16016	Helicopter Stabilized Hover Checks Before Departure
SAFO 17010	Incorrect Airport Surface Approaches and Landings
SAFO 19001	Landing Performance Assessments at Time of Arrival
STARs	Standard Terminal Arrival Routes
TPP	Terminal Procedures Publications
USCG Navigation Rules	USCG Navigation Rules, International-Inland
VFR Navigation Charts	Sectional/Terminal Aeronautical Charts

Section 6: Abbreviations and Acronyms

Note: Users should reference the current edition of the reference documents listed below. The current edition of all FAA publications can be found at www.faa.gov.

Acronym	Description
14 CFR	Title 14 of the Code of Federal Regulations
AATD	Advanced Aviation Training Device
AC	Advisory Circular
ACS	Airman Certification Standards
ADM	Aeronautical Decision-Making
ADS-B	Automatic Dependent Surveillance Broadcast
ADS-C	Automatic Dependent Surveillance - Contract
AFCS	Automatic Flight Control System
AFM	Airplane Flight Manual
AGL	Above Ground Level
AIM	Aeronautical Information Manual
AIRMET	Airman's Meteorological Information
AKTR	Airman Knowledge Test Report
AMEL	Airplane Multiengine Land
AMES	Airplane Multiengine Sea
APU	Auxiliary Power Unit
ASEL	Airplane Single-Engine Land
ASES	Airplane Single-Engine Sea
ASI	Aviation Safety Inspector
ATC	Air Traffic Control
ATD	Aviation Training Device
ATP	Airline Transport Pilot
BATD	Basic Aviation Training Device
CDI	Course Deviation Indicator
CDL	Configuration Deviation List
CFIT	Controlled Flight Into Terrain
CFR	Code of Federal Regulations
CG	Center of Gravity
CPDLC	Controller–pilot data link communication
CRM	Crew Resource Management
DA	Decision Altitude
DDA	Derived Decision Altitude

Acronym	Description
DH	Decision Height
DME	Distance Measuring Equipment
DP	Departure Procedures
EFB	Electronic Flight Bag
EFC	Expect Further Clearance
EFIS	Electronic Flight Instrument System
ELT	Emergency Locator Transmitter
ETA	Estimated Time of Arrival
ETL	Effective Translational Lift
FAA	Federal Aviation Administration
FAF	Final Approach Fix
FB	Wind and Temperature Aloft Forecast
FFS	Full Flight Simulator
FMS	Flight Management System
FRAT	Flight Risk Assessment Tool
FSB	Flight Standardization Board
FSO	Flight Standards Office
FSTD	Flight Simulation Training Device
FTD	Flight Training Device
G	Unit of Force Equal to Earth's Gravity
GBAS	Ground Based Augmentation System
GFA	Graphical Forecast for Aviation
GNSS	Global Navigation Satellite System
GPS	Global Positioning System
H/V	Height/Velocity
HF	High Frequency
HIGE	Hover in Ground Effect
HUD	Head Up Display
IFR	Instrument Flight Rules
ILS	Instrument Landing System
IMC	Instrument Meteorological Conditions
INFO	Information for Operators
INS	Inertial Navigation System
IOS	Instructor Operating Station
KOEL	Kinds of Operations Equipment List
L/DMAX	Lift/Drag Maximum

Acronym	Description
LAHSO	Land and Hold Short Operations
LNAV	Lateral Navigation
LOA	Letter of Authorization
LOC-I	Loss of Control in Flight
LP	Localizer Performance
LTE	Loss of Tail Rotor Effectiveness
LTM	Long Term Memory
MAP	Missed Approach Point
MDA	Minimum Descent Altitude
MEL	Minimum Equipment List
METAR	Aviation Routine Weather Reports (Meteorological Aerodrome Report)
MFD	Multi-Function Display
MMO	Maximum Operating Limit Speed as a Mach Number
NAS	National Airspace System
NOTAM	Notice to Air Missions
Nr	Main Rotor Speed
NSP	National Simulator Program
NTSB	National Transportation Safety Board
ODP	Obstacle Departure Procedure
OEI	One Engine Inoperative
PAVE	Risk Management Checklist for Pilot/Aircraft/enVironment/External Factors
PFD	Primary Flight Display
PIC	Pilot-in-Command
PinS	Copter Point in Space
PIREP	Pilot Report
POA	Plan of Action
POH	Pilot's Operating Handbook
PTS	Practical Test Standards
QPS	Qualification Performance Standard
QRH	Quick Reference Handbook
RAIM	Receiver Autonomous Integrity Monitoring
RCAM	Runway Condition Assessment Matrix
RFM	Rotorcraft Flight Manual
RNAV	Area Navigation
RNP	Required Navigation Performance
RPM	Revolutions Per Minute

Acronym	Description
SAE	Specialty Aircraft Examiner
SAFO	Safety Alert for Operators
SATR	Special Air Traffic Rules
SBAS	Satellite Based Augmentation System
SBT	Scenario Based Training
SFAR	Special Federal Aviation Regulation
SFRA	Special Flight Rules Area
SID	Standard Instrument Departure
SIGMET	Significant Meteorological Information
SMS	Safety Management System
SRM	Single-Pilot Resource Management
SRM	Safety Risk Management
STAR	Standard Terminal Arrival
STM	Short Term Memory
SUA	Special Use Airspace
TAF	Terminal Area Forecast
TAWS	Terrain Awareness and Warning System
TCAS	Traffic Collision Avoidance System
TCDS	Type Certificate Data Sheet
TCE	Training Center Evaluator
TEM	Threat and Error Management
TFR	Temporary Flight Restrictions
TPP	Terminal Procedures Publication
TUC	Time of Useful Consciousness
UHF	Ultra High Frequency
UIMC	Unintended Instrument Meteorological Conditions
USCG	United States Coast Guard
UTC	Coordinated Universal Time
V_1	The maximum speed in the takeoff at which the pilot must take the first action (e.g., apply brakes, reduce thrust, deploy speed brakes) to stop the airplane within the accelerate-stop distance. V_1 also means the minimum speed in the takeoff, following a failure of the critical engine at V_{EF}, at which the pilot can continue the takeoff and achieve the required height above the takeoff surface within the takeoff distance.
V_2	Takeoff Safety Speed
V_A	Maneuvering speed
VDP	Visual Descent Point
VFR	Visual Flight Rules

Acronym	Description
V_{MC}	Minimum control speed with the critical engine inoperative
VHF	Very High Frequency
VMC	Visual Meteorological Conditions
V_{MCG}	Minimum control speed on the ground with the critical engine inoperative
V_{MO}	Maximum Operating Limit Speed
V_{NE}	Never exceed speed
VCOA	Visual Climb Over Airport
VOR	Very High Frequency Omnidirectional Range
V_R	Rotation speed
V_{REF}	Reference Landing Speed
VRS	Vortex Ring State
V_S	Stall Speed
V_{SO}	Stalling Speed or the Minimum Steady Flight Speed in the Landing Configuration
V_{SSE}	Safe, intentional one-engine-inoperative speed. Originally known as safe single-engine speed
VTOL	Vertical Takeoff and Landing
V_X	Best angle of climb airspeed
V_{XSE}	Best angle of climb speed with one engine inoperative
V_Y	Best rate of climb speed
V_{YSE}	Best rate of climb speed with one engine inoperative.
WAAS	Wide Area Augmentation System

Section 7: Practical Test Checklist (Applicant)

Evaluator's Name: _____

Location: _____

Date/Time: _____

Acceptable Aircraft

☐ Aircraft Documents:

    ☐ Airworthiness Certificate

    ☐ Registration Certificate

    ☐ Operating Limitations

☐ Aircraft Maintenance Records:

    ☐ Logbook Record of Airworthiness Inspections and Airworthiness Directives (AD) Compliance

☐ Pilot's Operating Handbook and FAA-Approved Aircraft Flight Manual

Personal Equipment

☐ View-Limiting Device

☐ Current Aeronautical Charts (printed or electronic)

☐ Computer and Plotter

☐ Flight Plan Form and Flight Logs (printed or electronic)

☐ Chart Supplements, Airport Diagrams, and Appropriate Publications (printed or electronic)

☐ Current AIM (printed or electronic)

Personal Records

☐ Government-Issued Identification—Photo/Signature Identification (ID)

☐ Pilot Certificate

☐ Current Medical Certificate or BasicMed Qualification (when applicable)

☐ Completed FAA Form 8710-1, Airman Certificate and/or Rating Application, or completed IACRA form, FAA Form 8710-11, Airman Certificate and/or Rating Application—Sport Pilot, or FAA Form 8400.3, Airman Certificate and/or Rating Application with Instructor's Signature, if applicable

☐ Airman Knowledge Test Report

☐ Airman's Logbook with Appropriate Instructor Endorsements

☐ FAA Form 8060-5, Notice of Disapproval (if applicable)

☐ Letter of Discontinuance (if applicable)

☐ Approved School Graduation Certificate (if applicable)

Section 8: Knowledge Test Reports and Archived ACS Codes

Private Pilot for Airplane Category ACS Archived Codes

PA.III.A.R3	Confirmation or expectation bias.
PA.IV.A.S10	Retract the water rudders, as appropriate, establish and maintain the most efficient planing/liftoff attitude, and correct for porpoising and skipping (ASES, AMES).
PA.IV.I.S5	Retract the water rudders as appropriate; advance the throttle smoothly to takeoff power.
PA.IV.K.S7	Retract the water rudders as appropriate; advance the throttle smoothly to takeoff power.
PA.VIII.E.K1a	Sensitivity, limitations, and potential errors in unusual attitudes
PA.VIII.E.K1b	Correlation (pitch instruments/bank instruments)
PA.VIII.E.K1c	Function and operation
PA.VIII.E.K1d	Proper instrument cross-check techniques
PA.VIII.E.R2	Failure to seek assistance or declare an emergency in a deteriorating situation.
PA.VIII.E.R6	Failure to unload the wings in recovering from high G situations.
PA.VIII.F.S3	Maintain altitude ±200 feet, heading ±20°, and airspeed ±10 knots.
PA.IX.C.K1a	Maintain altitude ±200 feet, heading ±20°, and airspeed ±10 knots
PA.IX.C.K1b	Engine roughness or overheat
PA.IX.C.K1c	Loss of oil pressure
PA.IX.C.K1d	Fuel starvation
PA.XII.A.R2	Confirmation or expectation bias as related to taxi instructions.
PA.XII.A.S1	Demonstrate runway incursion avoidance procedures.
PA.XII.B.R2	Confirmation or expectation bias as related to taxi instructions.

Commercial Pilot for Airplane Category ACS Archived Codes

CA.I.F.K2f	Weight and balance
CA.IV.A.S10	Retract the water rudders, as appropriate, establish and maintain the most efficient planing/liftoff attitude, and correct for porpoising and skipping (ASES, AMES).
CA.IV.I.S5	Retract the water rudders as appropriate; advance the throttle smoothly to takeoff power.
CA.IV.K.S7	Retract the water rudders as appropriate; advance the throttle smoothly to takeoff power.
CA.IV.B.S5	Recognize signal loss or interference and take appropriate action, if applicable.
CA.IX.C.K1a	Engine roughness or overheat
CA.IX.C.K1b	Carburetor or induction icing
CA.IX.C.K1c	Loss of oil pressure
CA.IX.C.K1d	Fuel starvation
CA.XI.A.R2	Confirmation or expectation bias as related to taxi instructions.
CA.XI.A.S1	Utilize runway incursion avoidance procedures.
CA.XI.B.R2	Confirmation or expectation bias as related to taxi instructions.

Instrument Rating – Airplane ACS Archived Codes

IR.IV.B.R2	Failure to recognize an unusual flight attitude and follow the proper recovery procedure.
IR.VII.C.R2	Collision hazards, to include aircraft, terrain, obstacles, wires, vehicles, vessels, persons, and wildlife.

Airline Transport Pilot and Type Rating ACS Archived Codes

AA.IV.B.R2	Failure to recognize an unusual flight attitude and follow the proper recovery procedure.
AA.V.A.S2	When accomplished in an FSTD, the entry should be consistent with the expected operational environment for a stall on takeoff or while on approach in a partial flap configuration with no minimum entry altitude defined.
AA.V.B.S2	When accomplished in an FSTD, the entry should be consistent with the expected operational environment for a stall in cruise flight with no minimum entry altitude defined.
AA.V.C.S2	When accomplished in an FSTD, the entry should be consistent with the expected operational environment for a stall when fully configured for landing with no minimum entry altitude defined.
AA.VI.F.R3	Planning for.
AA.VI.F.R3a	a. Missed Approach
AA.VI.F.R3b	b. Land and hold short operations (LAHSO)
AA.VI.H.R3	Planning for.
AA.VI.H.R3a	a. Missed Approach
AA.VI.H.R3b	b. Land and hold short operations (LAHSO)
AA.VIII.A.R2	Confirmation or expectation bias as related to taxi instructions.
AA.VIII.B.R2	Confirmation or expectation bias as related to taxi instructions.